ORIENTATION

THE BENCHMARKS SERIES

KATE CANTERBARY

VESPER PRESS

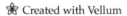 Created with Vellum

ABOUT ORIENTATION

Max Murphy's no-fail plan for kicking this year's ass and getting his life back on track:

1. Forget about the cheating ex. Forget all about him. No more sad sack moping. None of that downer vibe. None of it.
2. Look for a new place to live in order to move out of my sister's basement. Free digs are great but killing my sex life.
3. Return the intramural softball league to glory and greatness.
4. Fall in fresh, lusty love with Jory Hayzer, the hot new science teacher the minute I see him and his sexy Superman hair.
5. Get the hot science teacher on my trivia team. Couples who play together stay together.
6. Spend an entire school year wooing the very

hot but also very skittish science teacher. Fall in hard, crazy love with him in the process.

7. Freak out, screw it all up, and hope to hell there's a way to make it right.

PART I

SUMMER

1

JORY

LATE, late, late, late, late. How the hell am I this late?

If you asked my mother, she'd tell you I did this in varying degrees every year. She'd say it started in preschool, right around the time I was able to fully comprehend the notion of a new school year. I'd stalk the mailbox for my teacher assignment. I'd stay awake for days at a time, agonizing over which friends might be in my class. Lists upon lists of school supplies. An entire week was earmarked for breaking in shoes, trying on outfits, loading and unloading my backpack, timing my morning get-ready routine.

She'd say my fits of new school year fastidiousness were the product of my perfectionism, my Type A personality, my anxious disposition. Even at four years old, I'd possessed all three the way I'd possessed my skin and bones and blood.

If you asked me, I'd say the first days of school neuroses were passed down to me like a vintage pair of penny loafers. My mother was a teacher. She'd spent thirty years—and counting—in the company of Portsmouth, New Hampshire's fourth graders and no one was more high-strung come the end of summer than her. And that was a noteworthy feat considering my divorce attorney sister was a lifelong insomniac who survived on little more than iced coffee, Twizzlers, and the souls of those fools who dared to cross her.

Regardless of the origin of my issues, they were mine and they visited every August, but they didn't look the same these days. At twenty-nine years old, I still obsessed over class rosters and supply lists and morning routines. The hunt for the perfect pair of school shoes never ended. Now, my obsessions included taking apart my curriculum and putting it back together in an order that pleased me, organizing and reorganizing my classroom, and running an entire quarter's worth of copies before the first day of school.

And, apparently, showing up late for the start of teacher in-service at my new school.

"Seriously. How the hell did I manage this?" I mumbled as I slammed the car door shut and sprinted toward the building. In Boston's soupy August heat, I knew running in my trousers, green gingham shirt, and funky tie meant I'd be sweaty and wrinkled before reaching the door. But then again—"Where the hell is the door?"

I skittered to a stop where I'd expected to find the main entrance. Instead of a handful of stairs and gleaming double doors, I found a pile of jackhammered rubble, plywood, and caution tape. No detour sign in sight.

I couldn't stomach another look at the time, instead swiveling my head from side to side in search of an alternative entry point. For lack of a better option, I headed toward the bus lane. I didn't remember enough of the building floor plan from my interview back in April to know where I was going, but after teaching in five different buildings over the past seven years, I knew there was always a door near the bus lane.

With every step, my jittery mind created increasingly ridiculous horror stories. Cutting through the in-progress meeting while my new colleagues watched me search for an empty seat like the sad fool who couldn't keep it professional for a single day. Finding my way into the building only to discover I had the date wrong, much to the annoyance of the school secretary. Having to climb in through a window and managing to come crashing down on the principal's desk. Sitting through a perfectly lovely professional development session only to get fired at the end of the day because I was incapable of arriving at work on time.

"Hey there."

"H-Hey," I stammered. I closed my fingers around the strap of my messenger bag as I glanced up at the wide slab of man in front of me. In the back of my mind—the section not consumed with keeping my job—I knew this man was all of my favorite things. Tall and broad, bronzed like a statue, and a smile so bright it rivaled the sun.

I was none of those things. I refused to speculate whether that made them my favorites.

"Need some help?" he asked.

My gaze landed on his polo shirt. Specifically, the way it hugged his shoulders as if testing the fabric's limits. The school crest was embroidered over his heart and that was a wonderful invitation to eye-fondle his chest. A ball cap shadowed his eyes, but I was certain he was blond underneath it. The golden fuzz on his forearms guaranteed it.

I could've spent all day cataloging the finest of his features, but I was still late. I stabbed a finger toward the building. "How do I get in?"

"They're not done with the front entrance yet, are they? Can't believe it's taking so long. At this rate, we'll have to catapult kids into the building."

If it was possible, his smile deepened as he mimed pulling back a catapult before launching it forward. The way his biceps flexed was...well, I ran a hand over my mouth to make sure I wasn't drooling.

"What can I help you with?" He gave me the kind of up-and-down that wasn't meant to bring goose bumps to my skin but succeeded nonetheless. "Are you here for the in-service? The one for new staff?"

I jerked my chin up in response before I could manage the word, "Yes." I didn't trust myself to offer more, not right now. It didn't matter whether he was the best thing about this entire city. I was late to my first day of work, and I couldn't screw this up. I needed this year to go well because I couldn't go looking for another teaching assignment in a few short months. I'd put everything on the line to get this job—and drained my savings to move here—and it needed to work.

"Well, that's great. Good to have you." He scooped a thick arm through the air as he turned toward the building. "Come on around back with me. I'll show you my best kept secret."

It took me a moment to shelve all thoughts of my big, helpful stranger's best kept secret and blink away from his tight backside as he moved down the sidewalk. I had to lengthen my strides to keep up.

"Are you, uh, do you—" I called to the strong line of his shoulders.

He shot a confused glance over his shoulder before slowing to match my pace. He yanked his ball cap off his head and raked his fingers through his—*I knew it!*—honey-blond hair. "What is the matter with me?" he asked, mostly to himself. He replaced the ball cap and met my gaze with a bashful grin, like a golden retriever guilty of wagging too hard and taking out an entire rosebush in the process. "Max Murphy. I teach health and phys ed." He smiled down at the sidewalk. "The kids call me Coach Maximum."

I couldn't help the laugh that broke loose. "I can imagine they do."

"Let me guess." Max cut a glance in my direction, still smiling. He tapped a finger against his lips as he hummed. His gaze dropped to my slim trousers. "Middle school, for sure. You don't crawl around or sit criss-cross-applesauce with the littles in those pants."

That earned him another laugh. "You're right about that."

Nodding, he studied my gingham shirt and tie printed with pink and blue crabs. It was too damn hot for ties, but in the continuing saga of my overpreparation for school, I'd reasoned it was better to arrive overdressed and leave with a tie balled in my pocket. "I'm going to say science."

I waved at my tie. "What? No evidence to support that inference? Math teachers never wear pastel crabs or something like that?"

Max shook his head as we rounded the building. "Nah," he replied, chuckling. "You're the only new middle grade teacher this year." He tugged a lanyard from his pocket and waved his key fob at a panel on the building. When the locks disengaged, he held the door open for me. "That, and you look like a science teacher."

I stepped into a blessedly cool, dark hallway, never more thankful for air-conditioning than I was right now. But I had to know—"Which part of me looks like a science teacher?"

I glanced at Max in time to see a wave of pink washing up his neck. "Um, I, uh, I'm not sure." He shrugged, his gaze darting toward my shirt and then away, anywhere but me and my sweat-wrinkled gingham. "The green, I guess. Green for science. Is that a thing? Do content areas have designated colors? I don't know why I thought that. That's dumb, right? It's dumb. Never mind."

We stood a shoulder's width apart, the hallway empty. Max tipped his head up, blinked at the dimmed lights in a way that suggested he'd only now noticed their absence. He ran a hand over his chest, still watching the ceiling. Every visible inch of him was large and solid, as if his body had decided he was meant to spend his days using it for sport long before his mind could form such an idea. I figured he was in his late twenties, maybe early thirties.

He swallowed, turned his attention back toward me, and smiled when he found me staring. Again, I worried about drool. Stubble shadowed his neck and jaw in an invitation I couldn't accept. Not today.

"I'm late," I said, giving him *this isn't what I want* hands and *please understand I'd rather sweat on a hot sidewalk all day if it meant staring at your ass in those shorts* eyes. "Can you show me where I'm supposed to be?"

"Right here," Max replied, his words sandpaper rough.

My lips parted as a starved sound panted out of me. I didn't know I'd gone from stressed to starved in the span of minutes, but here I was, confused and—and absolutely melting for this man. "I'm not sure what that means."

Max reached behind him, opening a door that led to another hallway. "Right here," he repeated. "The first door on your left is the library. That's where you're supposed to be."

I stared over his shoulder as I gathered up the fragile, needy parts of myself I'd let go uncaged in the minutes since meeting Max. I didn't know what I was thinking. Rather, I hadn't thought. I'd followed this big, sweet golden retriever even when I knew better.

"Thank you," I said, not quite meeting his eyes. He leaned back against the door, making way for me to pass, but only if I angled my body. I didn't do that. I shuffled past him, the entire length of my arm brushing his chest as I went. Hard, hard, hard he was. I fixed my gaze on the buttons open at his throat, wondered whether I'd find him smooth or fuzzy if I slipped my hand under the fabric. Yeah, he was fuzzy. I was as positive as a proton about that. "It wasn't dumb."

"What?" he asked, the word barely more than a cough.

I risked a glance at his face. The smile remained but it didn't reach his eyes. "Green for science. It wasn't dumb. I think that too. That's...that's exactly why I wear it."

I couldn't surrender another minute to this man, not even if I wanted more than anything to do precisely that. Tightening my grip on the strap of my messenger bag, I marched toward the library.

"You're not late," Max called. "We always hold the first half hour for coffee and bagels. We're big into the coffee and bagel scene around here." He paused, probably waiting for me to turn and acknowledge his words with something more than a relieved exhale. Then, "Do you like bagels?"

I lifted my shoulders, let them fall. "Cinnamon raisin, yeah. Warmed, but not all the way toasted."

He made a noise that sounded like approval, a rumbling murmur that said, "Yes. Just like that."

"I like sesame, even if the seeds make a damn mess." He studied the front of his shirt, as if he expected he'd discover errant seeds there. "But I might try that cinny raisin some time."

"You should." I glanced back at him. "I'm Jory. Hayzer. Jory Hayzer."

His brows furrowed as he worked out my name in his head. There was no hiding these machinations as they were splashed all over his face. "Jory. Like Rory, but with a J."

I bobbed my head. "Yeah."

His smile could've thawed ice. It was possible he was thawing *my* ice as we spoke. "I like it."

"Thanks." Smiling wasn't my nature. It always looked like I was forced or uncomfortable. Slight grins were more my speed. But somewhere between my perfectionism and stoicism and ever-present anxiety, I found a true smile for Max. "Thank you for showing me the way," I said. "I should get in there. I need to assess the bagel situation."

His eyes turned stony and his lips flattened into a striking line as he jabbed a finger in my direction. "Defend that cinny raisin territory, Hayzer."

Max delivered that order as if he was calling plays from the sidelines. Serious, stern, allowing no room for argument. I adored it. *Adored it.* I couldn't decide whether it was my unanswered desire for a strong, certain presence at my side or the knowledge Max possessed as much strength as he did sweetness.

"I'll do that," I promised, still smiling.

The stern façade dissolved. "If you wanted, you could come find me after your new staff sessions today. I'll be around all day." He propped a hand on his waist, shrugged. If this was his way of affecting casual, it was even more adorable than the no-nonsense coach vibe. "It's mostly administrative stuff. Ordering supplies, organizing athletics schedules, sorting balls." He smirked. "Phys ed teachers. We've got a lot of balls."

"I bet you do," I replied, a laugh thick in my words. "And where should I find you and your balls?"

"In the closet."

I blinked. Once, twice. "Excuse me?"

The smirk deepened. "That's where they keep me around here. In the closet." Max gestured to the dark hallway. "My office is the phys ed supply closet. The imagery isn't lost on me."

At that, I laughed out loud. "I believe you mean the irony."

He snapped his fingers, pointed at me as he bobbed his head. "Yeah, that. *Irony.*"

"Is that something I should be aware of here?" I swept a glance down the hall, adding, "The closet and such?"

Pausing, he gifted me another up-and-down look. "This is a good place. Good people. Everyone is welcome here and we make a point of it. I've been at Bayside since the doors opened and I've never regretted it." His gaze locked onto my belt buckle before meeting my eyes. "Like I said, come find me later. I'll show you around and introduce you to the good copier and tell you anything you want to know about this school. Or anything else."

His words loosened something inside me. Something buried deep, far past the brittle overgrowth of cynicism and distrust. "I might do that, Coach."

2

MAX

SIX HOURS after watching Jory step into the library, my hands were still shaking.

Shaking.

I'd made four completely unnecessary trips to the front office in that time. All on the off chance of catching a glimpse of him while strolling past the library. But the problem with doors and walls was I couldn't see through them.

I didn't need much. Just one look at Jory, one clear-eyed look. I had to see that green, checkered shirt and Superman hair. I needed to confirm he was all right, to see for myself that the worried gleam in his eyes and apprehensive twist of his lips was gone. I couldn't explain why my gut churned with an unbearable urge to guard and protect him from anything that might cause him distress.

I couldn't explain it, but that was how I felt.

And I had a million questions for Jory. Maybe more. I wanted to know what he ate for lunch and whether he had a favorite Premier League team. I wanted to know why he liked teaching middle school science and if he wanted to carpool. I wanted to know if he wore glasses because I'd noticed a faint tan line at his temples, and I needed to prepare myself for the gut-punch of sexy nerd glasses along with his impatient frowns, the flawless light olive skin, and all that gorgeous Superman hair. And more than anything else, I wanted to know whether someone held a claim on him. I needed to know what I was up against.

I leaned back in my desk chair, bouncing my hands against the armrests as I watched the clock. That, plus some pointless pacing, was all I'd accomplished today. No ordering, no organizing, no sorting.

I'd made a solid effort at paging through a phys ed supply catalog around noon, but one look at a kit of over-sized bowling pins had me calling up an old-fashioned candlepin bowling alley and asking about their hours. Something told me Jory, with his weird crab tie, would like the vintage vibe.

Jory and anyone else from the staff I could gather for bowling and beers, of course. Unless Jory wanted to keep it small. Just the two of us.

"Oh my god, stop it," I said to myself. I rolled my chair away from the desk, braced my elbows on my thighs, and dropped my head into my hands. I had to stop. I couldn't keep fueling this fantasy fire. We'd talked for *minutes*. For all I knew, Jory was being polite and I was inventing all of this. I always did that. I invented things and jumped ten steps ahead and fell before there were feelings to fall into, and I stayed there like an overturned turtle long after realizing I'd fallen for all the wrong reasons. "Stop, stop, *stop*."

A knock sounded behind me, and then, "Is this a bad time?"

Oh my *god*. I dropped my hands and jerked out of my chair with a force that sent it crashing into a tower of stacked soccer nets. They skittered to the side, knocking over a pillar of orange safety cones and a bag of softballs, sending both straight for Jory's head.

"What is wrong with me?" I panted, diving in front of him to snatch the bag and steady the cones before they flattened him on the floor. I gained control of the equipment before it could do any damage, but I'd also shaved a few years off my life.

"Sorry. Didn't mean to sneak up on you like that." Jory folded his lips together and blinked away from me. "Thanks for intervening, though. You've got some reflexes."

I settled my hands on my waist and blew out a ragged breath. Jory was here in my office, wearing adorable dark-rimmed glasses and just being perfect while my hot mess of athletic equipment almost welcomed him with a concussion. "I didn't hear anything you just said because I'm still reliving the moment when a sack of softballs went flying toward your head."

"You did warn me about phys ed teachers and all their

balls." Jory ducked his head, laughing. "How about that tour?"

———

AT THE HEAD of the hallway, I spread my hands out in front of me. "Welcome to the land of short people, also known as the elementary floor." I motioned to the doors closest to us. "This end is early elementary. That's Zucconi's room. She's kindergarten." I pulled open the door, glanced inside. "I'm surprised Shay isn't here today. She's usually the first one in the building when we get the all-clear to start classroom setup."

"Is that common?" Jory asked. "Do teachers spend a lot of time on preparation?"

Crossing the hall, I shrugged. "It varies. Some like to spend a lot of time in their rooms. Others take work home. The language arts and history teachers spend every Sunday together, working on plans and coordinating curriculum. They hate each other, Clark and Noa, but they do it because they want everything aligned."

"I think I met Noa when I visited for my interview last spring," Jory said, tipping his head to the side as he considered this. Why did he have to be so smart and wonderful? It hurt to stand here and not rub my thumb over his brow just to feel his thoughts. "Yeah. She's a little shorter than me, black hair, beautiful golden skin?"

I opened the next door. "That's Noa Elbaz for you. We'll swing by her room and Clark Kerrin's too, but I doubt they're here. They always work on lesson plans at her place." I gestured to the pristine classroom. "This is Jaime Rouselle's classroom. She's first grade and the first one here in the morning, but she doesn't hang around in the afternoons. Jaime and Shay are best friends. Most of the time, their classes are working together on projects and have all kinds of flexible groups and it's a whole big thing. They're the nicest, happiest, most energetic people in the world."

Jory circled a cluster of desks. He was slim, several inches shorter than me, and a goddamn snack. Seriously, I'd never wanted to feel a man cozied up in my lap as badly as I wanted Jory. "Everything is so small."

I chuckled. "Don't let that fool you." When we returned to the hall, I pointed at two more doors. "Second and third grade are over here. Emme Ahlborg and Grace Kilmeade. Here's what you need to know about them: they're the exact opposites of Jaime and Shay."

He peered into Kilmeade's room, nodding solemnly. He did that a lot, the solemn nodding. He was a solemn guy, a serious guy. I was the polar opposite—as my ball jokes proved—but that wasn't going to be an issue for us. I'd had my share of good-time guys and the good times never lasted terribly long. Maybe it was time to get serious.

"Does that mean they're rude, disgruntled, and sedentary?"

"That's a good one, Hayzer." I rubbed the back of my neck. "No, they're wicked awesome teachers. The kids love them like crazy. But if Shay and Jaime are a piña colada, Emme and Grace are a Dark 'n' Stormy. You'll see what I mean when you meet them. They're all close friends and rock-star teachers, but they're also very different." I rubbed my neck again. Everything felt so damn *tight*. "If you're up for it, I could round up some people for a beer, maybe some bowling. We do that a lot around here. Maybe tonight? Or tomorrow, if that works better."

Jory bit his lower lip, glanced away. "I'll think about it. Okay? Today was—well, it was a lot. I'm trying to process everything, and I'm sure I have a ton of work to do setting up my room, and then there are a few more days of new teacher in-service before the rest of the staff returns and I'm just—"

"Hey." I rested my palm between his shoulder blades. Under that shirt, he was all tension. "Hey, hey. It's all good. There's plenty of time to meet everyone. We've got all year. Don't sweat it."

He gave me an unconvincing nod and my stomach twisted. What was I thinking? He'd probably spent the day being hit over the head with policies and protocols. The last thing he needed was forced socialization with his new colleagues.

"No, I'm sorry. You're being so helpful and I'm spinning out over nothing." He cut his hands through the air as if he was clearing away the things that troubled him. "I'd really dig a chance to meet everyone. I'm not great at bowling but—"

"I can help you with that," I interrupted. "Phys ed teachers can't help with much, but *bowling is our lane*."

Jory stared at me, his lips pursed as he fought back a smile. I wanted to kiss him more than anything. More than anything at all. I settled for keeping my hand on his back.

"Gym puns, huh?" he asked. I nodded, matching his grin. "Thank you for doing this. These little details really help me feel like I know what's going on here."

"You're welcome," I replied. We smiled at each other for so long, the motion sensitive lights above us turned off.

He glanced at the last two doors. "I guess we should keep moving."

I dropped my hand from his back. "Fourth and fifth grade. Audrey Saunders started out in fourth when she came here but moved up to fifth with her class a few years ago. Everyone loves Audrey because she's the sweetest lady ever and also because she brings in home-made cookies and cakes almost every week."

Jory patted his flat belly. "Audrey and I are going to be best friends."

"We have a new person in fourth grade. Elton or Eldon, I can't remember which one is correct."

His eyes brightened as he shifted to face me. "Tall, slender, Black guy? Yeah. I'm not sure if it's Eldon or Elton either but I met him today. He's a kickass teacher. Makes me want to go back to fourth grade."

"Can I ask you something?"

Jory nodded, stepped closer. I had to fold my arms over my chest to keep from dragging him even closer and finally, *finally* feeling him against me. "Yeah," he replied, a half smile pulling at his lips. "Go for it."

At some point during the day, he'd abandoned the tie

and opened the buttons at his throat. I couldn't stop staring at the exposed skin there. Not a freckle in sight. I'd never cared about the absence of freckles before but now it seemed like an opportunity, a challenge to study every inch of his skin. "What was your weird interview question?"

His brow furrowed. "What do you mean?"

"Lauren asks everyone a weird question," I answered, referring to Lauren Halsted-Walsh, the school principal. "There's always one bizarre, left-field question." Thinking back several years to my interview, I laughed. "She asked me how I'd handle a one-on-one conversation with a kid about body odor."

"Why would you have to handle a conversation like that?"

"As I've mentioned, I teach phys ed *and* health. I'm the one who gets to talk to these kids about their changing bodies. Or, that was how it was explained to me by Lauren. Keep in mind, I was twenty-four at the time, fresh out of student teaching, and on my third or fourth real job interview ever. Because scooping waffle cones at the old creamery in Needham did not require an extensive hiring process, you know?"

Jory snorted a laugh and my heart was pounding right out of my chest. "Okay, so how did you answer?"

"Oh, I didn't just answer the question," I said. "We *role-played* the conversation. She played the part of the shy-but-oblivious kid who hadn't discovered deodorant, and I played the part of the supportive coach who wanted to chat about good hygiene practices as we grew up. She asked random questions just like a sixth grader would. It was tough, man. Really tough. The whole time, I was convinced I wasn't getting the job."

"But, you did," he said.

"I mean, I'm here. I did something right," I replied. "Everyone has a weird interview question story, so I know you have one. Out with it, Hayzer."

He scratched his neck before answering. "She asked me what I'd do if I uncovered an underground slime ring. I wasn't completely clear what she was asking because the slime trade hasn't been an issue at any of my schools. I've dealt with water bottle flipping and Pokémon card hustlers, but not so much the slime. Once she painted the picture of a network of slime sellers all reporting to a slime kingpin, I understood."

"Oh, that's a good one. Last year's fifth graders were all about slime. You'll get plenty of that with your sixth grade class." I gestured for him to continue. "What was your brilliant response? Don't try to tell me it wasn't brilliant. I can tell you're a smart one."

Jory blushed. He actually blushed and I wanted to kiss every inch of that glow. Maybe it wasn't about the freckles or the glow but a runaway desire to kiss *him*, to explore *him*.

Forget ten steps ahead. I was a hundred steps ahead. A thousand.

"I proposed first identifying the key players and turning that information over to the administration," he said. "Then, conducting a lab experiment to explore the way bacteria living on slime multiplies when it exchanges hands with increasing frequency."

"Capitalizing on the gross factor. I like it." I stepped toward the staircase because I was going to touch him if I didn't. "I bet you want to see the middle grade hallway."

Jory followed me up the stairs. "You're right about that. I have a recurring nightmare about my classroom being a big pile of desks and chairs, a couple of beakers, and one uncalibrated scale. It's a recurring nightmare based in reality because I've inherited that situation a few times now."

When we reached the landing, I said, "You have nothing to worry about."

"I have everything to worry about," he murmured. "Always do."

I didn't know how to answer that. I didn't think he wanted me to pull him into my arms and promise everything would be all right, that I'd make it all right. I didn't think he wanted me to swear I'd do everything in my power to protect him.

"And this is the middle grade hall," I announced. "We try to keep the big kids contained, but the little ones come up here for art and music. Art is Linling Hsu and she's so freaking talented that it's scary. Music is Tiel Desai, also scary-talented. Like, seriously, she teaches third graders to play violin. How is that even real?"

Jory shook his head. "I don't know, but I love it. I can't wait to see that."

"The special needs folks have classrooms up here too. You probably met a few of them today since we're growing that team a lot this year." I motioned between a pair of doors across the hall from each other. "Noa Elbaz and Clark Kerrin are in here." Jory nodded, but I could tell he was trying to remember all the information I'd rattled off downstairs. "Language arts and history."

"Oh, right," he said, touching his fingertips to his forehead. He glanced at the other pair of doors. "Is this math and science?

"Yep. Juliana Avila is on the right. She's math. And this"—I pushed away from the wall and swung his door open—"is your new home."

He stepped into his classroom with his hands fisted at his sides. He didn't say anything for whole minutes —*minutes!*—as he studied the lab tables, books, shelves of equipment. It was the longest silence of my life, but as I watched the worry leave him like air from a balloon, I didn't mind it. If it was possible, I enjoyed it.

Perhaps I was exaggerating—getting ahead of myself again—but it seemed to me that Jory didn't make a habit of sharing things with others. I didn't know that for sure, though I'd noticed the way he'd pulled on a mask of complete calm when stepping into the library this morning. He'd shed the apprehension that had plagued him since the second I'd found him on the sidewalk, looking confused and miserable.

The truth was he hadn't shed that apprehension, not at all. He'd hidden it under a layer of cool control, one that almost read as boredom. He didn't bother with those layers and masks when he was with me.

Or, that was the story I wanted to believe. I wanted to

jump ten steps ahead. I wanted to be the one who absorbed his worry and cushioned his overwhelm. I wanted that and I'd want it until he told me otherwise.

"I'd put together a plan," he said, pacing in a small circle. "I had this plan written out with all the work I figured I'd need to do in order to be ready for the first day of school because I've always been stuck with the worst classrooms—if I even had a permanent classroom. I've always been the teacher bumped from one campus to another at the last damn minute and never had decent supplies." He waved at a glass cabinet filled with important-looking science-y things. "I don't know what to do if I don't need to spend the next week working on my plan. I'm good at preparing for the worst and getting through the worst, but I'm not good at adapting when the situation isn't that bad. I guess what I'm saying is, I don't know how to be relieved." He brought both hands to his temples. "I don't know why I'm dumping all of this on you, either. I'm sorry. I'm not one for talking about my emotions, but I can't seem to stop."

"You don't have to stop." I shrugged. Stuck my hands in my pockets. Pulled them out. Clasped them in front of me and then shook them out because it felt weird. Shifted from foot to foot. Then, "Since you have some free time, you could go bowling. With me."

Jory stopped pacing. "I'm not very good."

"I'll help you with that," I said. "Not that it matters. Beer and bowling are supposed to be fun, nothing else."

He moved toward me, stopping only when our shoes touched. "I think I'd like that, Max."

"I think I'd like..." My voice trailed off as I reached for him, my hand lingering a breath from his cheek until he granted me permission by tipping his head toward my touch. "I think I'd like to fall in love with you. If you'll let me."

He pressed his lips to my wrist and my knees damn near buckled. "I think I'd like to let you."

PART II

AUTUMN

3

JORY

A FULL MONTH.

That was how long it took me to take Max up on that date.

His patience was adorable. He invented excuses for me like he was an old pro at dealing with someone else's anxiety. Sometimes I wondered if he was.

Every time I sidestepped his offers and nearly burst into flames in the process, he made it all better with "No, you're right, you need time to unpack and settle into your apartment" and "Things are too hectic with the first weeks of school anyway" and "Forget I mentioned it. You need a minute to get into a groove. I'll be here whenever you're ready."

Max's excuses weren't too far removed from reality. Things were hectic and I was still living out of boxes in my apartment—not to mention learning how to cope with a roommate whose control freak tendencies were not part of the rental agreement—and my groove had thus far escaped me in the classroom.

But I didn't want him to go away. I didn't want him to stop asking me out.

When I'd first started teaching, I'd believed the school year would go well if the first days and weeks went well —and this was generally true. Setting the tone and establishing expectations right off the bat was essential, even if that thought process was catnip for my perfectionism. It made all my rituals and checklists even more important and built up those initial classes to do-or-die levels.

I knew better—somewhat—now. Imperfect starts didn't mean the year was going to be a disaster. It was okay for me and my classes to spend time getting to know each other and finding good vibes. And I didn't have to lock myself in my classroom for sixteen hours each day, reinventing my lesson plans, rearranging desks, and constructing mind-blowing experiments.

I could spare a minute to hang out with the cute coach...if that sort of thing wasn't triggering the shit out of my anxiety.

The fucked-up thing about anxiety was I couldn't say yes even when that was exactly what I wanted to do. Avoidance was always my first and most powerful instinct and I couldn't climb over it to let myself explore this connection with him. Avoidance was safe and secure, while exploration was an opportunity to get hurt, to be rejected, to prove anxiety right.

I didn't want anxiety to be right.

Irrational fears aside, I didn't want to be in the position of starting something with a new colleague only for it to blow up in my face before the end of the first marking period. I couldn't change schools or teaching assignments again. I could not handle that after several years of teaching in ever-changing grades and content areas.

The minute I thought I'd figured out physical science and sixth graders, I was switching over to eighth grade and life science. It didn't seem like a big deal but it was rather significant. Understanding the instructional goals and the ways that precise group of kids learned best required practice. Bouncing between grades and contents meant I'd only practiced adapting.

On top of that, I didn't want to end up in a disciplinary meeting because I'd violated a fraternization policy. It came as a slight relief when the upper school dean Drew Larsen laughed off that issue.

"That's not a problem here," he said when I'd pulled him aside after a vertical alignment planning meeting for schoolwide science instruction. "If it were, I wouldn't be engaged to Miss Treloff right now."

"Oh," I replied. "I didn't—I didn't know that. Congratulations."

I couldn't decide whether I was horribly self-absorbed or everyone in this school was extremely proficient at keeping their personal affairs on the down low because I didn't notice anyone being more than friendly or polite. Yet the deans were engaged and everyone said Clark and Noa had big time feelings for each other.

Maybe I was self-absorbed. I did spend a lot of time in my head.

Drew glanced across the library to where Tara Treloff sat with Shay and Jaime, the kindergarten and first grade teachers. "Now you do."

I nodded. "Okay. Thanks."

"Make good choices, Hayzer," he added, still watching his fiancée. His gaze was cool, almost unemotional but it lingered long enough to prove it was anything but. How had I missed that before? "Be professional and keep it that way when you're around kids."

The green light from Drew got me around part of the anxiety.

The institutionalized happy hours closed the rest of the loop.

None of my previous schools maintained a happy hour tradition as robust as Bayside School's. Since I wasn't a big drinker and often found unstructured social events (and structured ones, for that matter) to be unnecessarily stressful, I'd skipped the first gathering. I liked to give my classroom a thorough organization at the end of the week and prep for the coming week anyway.

This didn't seem like a problem to me...until my colleagues started asking for a blood oath that I'd show up.

Clark, Noa, and Juliana had gone as far as to individually seek me out and insist the outing was mandatory for middle school team cohesion. A few of the elementary teachers caught me in the halls to ask if they'd see me on Friday afternoon. Max dropped by my classroom at least four times to confirm I was attending and then waited for me in the school parking lot to make sure I had good directions since I was new in town.

Talk about overwhelming. Part of me felt affronted by the hard sell but the other part percolated with the idea these people were trying to become my friends if I'd just let them. Could it be that easy?

In the end, I'd followed Max to the beer garden everyone seemed to love and shared a pint with my new coworkers. We had to look like a strange bunch, all of us drinking at four in the afternoon while decked out in jeans and college t-shirts because that was our school spirit custom for Fridays.

It didn't take long to realize this tradition wasn't about the beer as much as it was about the company. These people liked spending time together and they liked welcoming others into their common law family.

I had too much of a good time to hear the whispers and shouts of anxiety, and I joined them the next week, no blood oaths required.

The week after that, Max dropped onto the bench beside me as the September sun dipped into the horizon. I was happy to see him. Happy I'd had a month to get to know him beyond that sudden surge of heat and connection I'd felt the day we met. Happy I'd been able to find my homeostasis after navigating a huge season of change.

And I was happy to say yes when he asked, "What d'you say, Hayzer? Can I buy you dinner sometime?"

IT TOOK a full month for me to say yes and then another two weeks for us to arrive at a date and time. For once, it wasn't all my brain's fault. Since teachers didn't do weeknight outings—at least, not *this* teacher—we were limited to weekends and those were in short supply. Max was busy babysitting his sister's kids when she and her husband were away for an anniversary weekend. I was attending a training the next.

When we finally met up on a postcard perfect October afternoon, I thought I knew what I was getting myself into with Max.

I had no idea.

We met outside the gates of Fenway Park with a quick, slightly stiff hug where we lingered just long enough to make breaking apart awkward. I told myself it was awkward because we hadn't shared a minute without students or colleagues watching us and we had to learn how to do it right. I held his hand as I followed him inside the park.

Our seats were mediocre but it didn't matter because the sun was warm and bright and Max was completely magnetic. He talked nonstop, his opinions of the players and the action on the field wedged in between questions about me, chatter about our school, musings about fun spots we could visit in the city. And he did it all with his arm draped over the back of my seat like it'd always been there.

I liked that.

I liked hearing about his childhood Little League victories and his high school triumphs on the football field, going to school to teach phys ed because he'd always wanted to wear shorts and play dodgeball as a profession, his therapist sister Mallori and all the ways she routinely attempted to "shrink" him. And I liked telling him about all my new school year rituals, my decidedly non-athletic youth, how it seemed teaching was predestined for me and my comfortable acceptance of that. And as much as I could like an experience as rough and crumbly as shale, I liked that we both grew up without a father figure in our lives.

I liked it all so much I didn't object when he carted me to a nearby sports bar after the game. The home team had won and everyone was in such great spirits and he never, ever stopped touching me. No, I had *not* lodged an objection because I was too busy beaming at him with big, dreamy heart eyes.

And why did I need to object? I wasn't into the rowdy sports bar scene but I could manage this for a bit. A beer, some wings, whatever. I was with Max and that was all that mattered.

After an hour filled with mingling and recounting the best plays with the other sports fans packed into the loud, hot bar, Max leaned in close and said, "Let's get out of here."

I almost grabbed his stubbly face and kissed him.

I'd expected him to suggest going for a walk on the Esplanade or grabbing an ice cream cone or, hell, just calling it a night and going our separate ways because staying out this late wasn't the norm for my homebody soul. Instead of walking or ice cream, we ended up at the open-air playground for adults, the Lawn on D—and we were just in time for the live music to kick off.

"This band is killer," Max yelled over the noise.

He moved his body with the music and there was no denying he loved this. A significant portion of me wanted to tell him this was *not* killer, not for me, but he looped his arm around my waist and urged me to sway along with him. All the things that chafed and bothered like a clothing tag in a troublesome spot eased—this was different but not necessarily uncomfortable.

"Yeah," I replied, pushing up on my toes to speak into his ear. "Completely killer."

Max grinned down at me, his eyes smiling and his sun-bleached hair glowing white under the lights, and I decided I liked this man and his wild, overwhelming, noisy adventures very, very much.

I rested my hand between his shoulder blades and pressed him closer. "Kiss me," I said, glancing at his lips.

The music was too loud for Max to make out those words but the combination of my hand on his back and my gaze all over his mouth got the message across.

He cupped my jaw and swept his thumb over my lips. "I've been thinking about this," he said. "Imagined it a whole bunch of different ways."

"Did you imagine it like this?"

He blinked down at my mouth, nodding. For a second, it seemed he was poised to say something else, but then he lowered his head and sealed his lips over mine.

At first, I went rigid because even if my heart wanted

this, my head didn't trust anything new. Never did. Once I overcame that, everything fell into place. I granted myself permission to melt into him, to fall into his kiss like it was the one true place I belonged.

When Max pulled back, he brought his thumb to my lips. He studied me with his dark brown eyes as if he was contemplating something rather consequential. Then, "I really like you, Jory Hayzer. I like the way you taste and the way you kiss. I like the way you feel up against me."

Even at this close range, we still had to shout to hear each other, and I wasn't sure I understood everything Max was saying, but that didn't matter because I felt it. I felt the heat of his interest. The tight coil of his undivided attention. The burn of arousal low in my belly.

For the first time in an age, I was the object of someone's affection, and I enjoyed it more than I thought possible.

"Same here," I replied.

Max shifted me to face the stage and positioned himself behind me, his arms wrapped around my torso as he resumed swaying with the music.

Never in a million years would I have chosen an evening like this one for myself. My feet were sore. My throat was growing raw from all the shouting. There was a curious stain on the elbow of my sweater. And if I slowed down long enough to listen, I'd hear all the fears and worries and avoidance waiting for me on the other side of these good feelings.

But right now, there was nowhere else I wanted to be.

AFTER WATCHING the entire concert and lingering at the Lawn for a bit, Max and I hopped on the subway with the intention of finding a taco stand all the way up in Davis Square. Because that made sense.

"This doesn't make any sense," Max said as we filed onto a Red Line train with—apparently—half the population of Boston. And they were all drunk. "This is crazy. Where's everyone going?"

He led me to an open square of standing room at the end of the car. It wasn't much, but at least we could tuck ourselves up against the wall rather than jostling for room around one of the poles.

"Maybe they heard about the tacos too," I said.

Max wrapped his arms around me as a chime sounded and the train jerked forward. "I'll fight 'em off for you, babe."

With each stop, more passengers boarded and our corner of the car seemed to shrink. Somewhere between Downtown Crossing and Park Street Station, I found myself pressed into every ridge and groove of Max's body.

And, my god, that body was *hard*.

All at once, I realized my ass was shoved up against one hell of an erection and the sound in my ear was a low, ragged growl and his hands kept fisting and releasing the hem of my shirt.

And—for no other reason than wanting to—I rocked back against him.

A grunt snapped out of him, deep and harsh like a warning. "Watch it, Hayzer."

The chimes sounded again when the train rattled to a stop at Charles Street. Passengers forced their way in, driving us closer together. *Tighter. Harder.*

There were people everywhere and they were loud. Rowdy, even. And they were close enough for me to count their eyelashes and taste their beer breath. This was my least favorite part of public transit, though the cattle car anonymity of it all didn't bother me too much. Even if it should've cranked up my anxiety, it didn't. Just another reason brains were weird.

I squirmed a bit to avoid the person with the foul beer breath and—

"*Hayzer,*" Max growled.

Since I loved the irritated pinch in his voice and wanted to see if it looked as sexy as it sounded, I shifted to face him. As I moved, the train lurched and I lost my balance.

"Seriously, Hayzer." Max caught me around the waist, twisted me away from the beer breath, and hauled me up against his chest.

That was when I learned two things. One, his cock was unreal. That beast would split me in half and I'd thank him for it.

And two, I liked Max enough to let him. Maybe not right now, maybe not tonight. But someday.

"Is that big boy for me or do you have a thing for subways?" Max asked, his fingers splayed on the small of my back.

"It's not the subway," I said, my forehead dropping to his broad chest.

"Didn't think it was." He held himself still, leaving the train to stroke my body over his. Another stop—and another and another—came and went, the train jerking and chiming and lurching as if dry humping and depravity were on the the secret menu.

Max shifted his other hand to my waist, twisting his fingers around my belt. That subtle shift jerked my hips back, just enough for him to shove his thick thigh between my legs.

"Go ahead," he rasped into my ear. "Ride my leg. Show me how you get it, baby."

This train was too crowded—and too drunk—to notice anything out of the ordinary. I was certain we looked like any other couple locked in an embrace at the end of an exciting evening. It didn't matter whether every jolt and bump of the train drew a groan from my throat or deepened the flush washing over my face. It didn't matter whether I wanted Max to slip his hand under my clothes and stroke me with the same assertiveness he employed to grip my belt like it was a collar and grind my shaft up his thigh. I knew none of it mattered and I knew we could get away with it too.

"I have some bad news for you." He dragged his scruffy beard down my neck and I shivered into him. "Very bad news, babe."

"What's that?" I panted.

The chimes sounded again. The passengers shuffled toward the doors.

He bit my earlobe. "This is our stop."

I felt like I was going to burn from the inside out. Like I was going to turn into a human supernova. Like my body wasn't my own but a swollen bundle of need just waiting to be stroked, sucked, bitten—anything. *Anything.*

It made me dizzy and delirious, and I didn't pay any attention to where we were going. Max led the way, ordered the tacos, sat me on a bench with orders to drink a bottle of water while we waited for our food.

Never in my life had I been reduced down to the demands of my dick. Sure, it had made its desires known but this...this was torture.

"—and my friend Joseph does this cool thing where he and his partner host these nights, like Spanish night or French night or whatever. They call it 'Eat the Globe' and we only speak Spanish or French while we're there and we eat Spanish or French food. It's awesome. You'll meet them soon. They're awesome. They're the best guys. Oh, and trivia nights. I bet you're a boss at trivia. You are going to *adore* Tom. Maybe we could go next week. What d'you think?"

I paused, my taco an inch from my mouth. "Wait—what? Where are we going next week?"

It was after midnight. We'd been together—and having a great though exhausting, sexually frustrating time—since the afternoon. It would be another hour before I was back at my Quincy apartment. And now we were penciling in plans for next weekend? I wasn't sure I'd be fully recovered by then.

"To trivia." Max glanced over at me from his side of

the park bench we'd chosen for this late-night taco supper. "It's at the best little tavern and—"

I set the taco down, wiped my hands, and stared at the ground as I tuned out the finer points of Max's friend group trivia traditions. I didn't know how to explain to someone I liked and wanted to spend more time with that I'd had fun but this was not my normal. I was willing to step beyond the bounds of my comfort zone—and those avoidant tendencies—but I couldn't do that every single weekend and be a functional teacher during the week. I didn't operate on the same fuel as Coach Maximum—I needed downtime and quiet and a heavy pour of predictability.

I rubbed my forehead. "Max. Listen."

"Yeah?" He leaned closer, dipped his head to catch my gaze. "What's up?"

He looked so sweet. *So sweet.* And concerned. He peered at me like he truly wanted to hear what I had to say, and I just didn't think I could bear to dim the light in his eyes. Not on my stupid, anxious, fretful account.

"You're right. I am into trivia," I said. "That sounds incredible and so do your friends. Sign me up for French night. I'll bring the brie en croute."

"But? Because I heard the but."

"But…" I trailed off. I wasn't good at articulating my needs. I wasn't good at disagreeing or saying no, even when it was in my best interest. I didn't like making my issues someone else's problem—not being a problem was a core principle of my anxiety—though I had the strange sense Max could handle my problems. That he'd be offended if I didn't share them. "But you should know my bedtime is ten p.m., and on most school nights, I'm tucked in with a book by nine. I had an amazing time, Max, fully amazing, though I'm not sure I'll ever be able to pack a baseball game and a concert, plus stops at a sports bar and a Somerville taco stand into one date again."

"I went a little overboard, huh?"

I replied with a shrug-nod. "I had an amazing time," I repeated. "But I'm gonna need some hot tea and a lazy day in bed after all this."

"I can accommodate those needs," Max replied, his gaze heating.

"Max…"

He laughed, but I knew he was serious. If I agreed, he'd escort me to his bed and keep me there the remainder of the weekend. In many ways, I wanted that. I wanted to be with Max, to open myself up to him in every way, to get lost in him. But I also wanted to be cautious with him. This wasn't a race and there was no penalty for taking it slow.

And I was pretty sure I'd developed a blister on one of my toes. There was nothing sexy about that.

"As nice as that sounds, I don't think I'm ready to add that to today's adventure. I'm too tired to be polite—"

"I don't allow good manners in my bed anyway," he interrupted.

"You know, Max," I started as I dropped my head on his shoulder, "that doesn't surprise me."

4

MAX

I PULLED a navy blue sweater over my head, immediately whipped it off, and added it to the pile forming on my bed. Wrong. All wrong.

My wardrobe consisted of t-shirts, polo shirts, and sweatshirts. My non-gym-teacher apparel was limited. And all of it was wrong.

"This would be easier if I had a damn clue where we were going," I grumbled to myself.

Since I'd turned our first date into a chapter from *The Hobbit*, I suggested Jory plan the next outing. That way, he was guaranteed to enjoy himself, and I'd learn what he liked. Because I obviously had no clue and when I'd tried to feel him out before our first date, he'd insisted he was up for anything. He'd repeated that sentiment the whole night too.

I wasn't the sharpest tack in the box, and sometimes I failed to read between the lines, but I'd checked in a bunch of times that night and he'd given me every indication of having a wicked good time. I'd realized at the taco stand that some of his smiles were more like grimaces and it seemed to me he'd only let those slip by because I'd put him through a marathon of fun and he was too tired to censor himself.

No more of that. Nope. It should've dawned on me while I'd asked him out a half dozen times only for him to respond with wide, overwhelmed eyes, fidgety hands, and a gentle change of topic. Jory liked slow. He needed it that way—and I had to adjust accordingly. It didn't matter whether my whole body clenched when he smiled or I got a massive endorphin rush from seeing his name in my text message inbox. Jory favored a slower, steadier approach and it was on me to adapt.

Tonight, I'd make sure he was tucked into bed right on time. I wasn't opposed to doing the tucking—I'd tuck the fuck out of him—but there was no need to rush.

In fact, rushing wasn't even a concern at all as I couldn't find a single thing to wear. I tossed another sweater on the bed and headed toward the staircase leading up to the main level of my sister's house.

"Mallori," I called. "Can you help me?"

I lived with my sister—and her husband and kids.

"With what?" she shouted back.

The basement wasn't so much an apartment but a dark, slightly damp dungeon with a small bathroom that leaned hard enough into rustic chic that my niece and nephew were terrified of stepping a single toe in there. But it was free and free was a bangin' deal.

I leaned back against the wall. "I don't know what to wear."

She made a sound, one that conveyed frustration, impatience, and grudging affection all at once and carried through walls and ceilings with ease. It was the knuckle-ball of mom sighs because it was never clear which of those emotions would connect the hardest.

"Jeans and a nice sweater," she replied.

I shot a baleful glance at the pile on my sofa bed. "I don't have any nice sweaters," I yelled.

We were yellers. We might not have been born this way but we grew up that way and hadn't managed to outgrow it yet.

"Oh my god," she muttered as she jogged down the stairs from the kitchen. "I gave you a nice sweater last Christmas, and the kids gave you one for your birthday a couple of years ago. What's wrong with those options?" She gave my boxer briefs the *why are you practically naked* mom sigh before turning her attention to the bed. "What's this all about?"

"I have a date," I said.

"Really? You kids still use the word *date*? That's neat."

My sister was barely two years older than me yet treated that gap like two decades. She was always the adult in our relationship. Always the smart one, the mature one, the sensible one, the settled one—and she knew it.

I was...none of those things. I lived here because I'd had nowhere else to go when things with Teddy fell all the way apart last winter. Walking into our apartment and finding him with another man *on my birthday* was the last and final straw. There'd been other last straws, too many to count, and I was ashamed of each one of them because I'd put up with Teddy being terrible to me for much longer than I could cover up with excuses.

I glared at her as she picked through my pile. "I don't know about the other *kids* but yeah, I'm calling it a date, Mallori."

"It's clear you're not going down to Dedham House of Pizza with this amount of drama." She snorted and plucked the navy sweater from the heap. "This is cute. Wear this and don't stress."

I folded my arms over my chest. "I'm not interested in cute."

"Be cute and be happy about it," she said, tossing me the sweater. "This shows off your tan."

To Mallori, there was nothing better than a good, lasting tan. She was known to drag a lawn chair out in March, all bundled up in a winter coat, just to catch some rays on her face.

"It's not—" I held up the sweater, wishing she could understand my distress. "It's just *not.*"

I didn't know where Jory would want us to go, but I knew this sweater wasn't right. He was always talking about the books and journals he read, the podcasts he listened to, the documentaries he watched. He'd want to go somewhere intellectual like that—maybe a museum or a symposium. I didn't know what a symposium actually involved but it seemed like something he'd enjoy.

Or a symphony. Did I have anything appropriate for a symphony?

No. Definitely not.

"Okay. I know that look. You're freaking out. We need to pull it back in, Coach." She dropped her hands on my biceps, gave me a firm squeeze. "Step one: where are you going on this date?"

I shook out of her hold and raked my hands through my hair, which was now fully fucked up. "I don't know!"

"Oh." She squinted at me as I paced the short length of the basement. "Then…why don't you call him and find out?"

"Because I'm trying to be easy," I replied, shrugging as if nothing could possibly bother me. "I'm trying to go with the flow. I'm trying to be low maintenance."

"Did he give you the impression you needed to be low maintenance in order to spend time with him?"

I picked up a pair of jeans and smoothed out the legs. "No."

Mallori blew out a breath as she rubbed her temples. "This little situation we're having right now should inform you that approach isn't working. You're sacrificing your boundaries to meet the needs you've assigned to someone else. You're letting yourself slip into second position again because that pattern is familiar and it feels safe but you know it's not. You know you deserve to be as high maintenance as your emotions require, and if he can't hack that, he's not right for you."

Did I mention my sister was a marriage and family therapist? Because yeah.

"Okay, Mal, I get it." I reached for another pair of jeans. "But I have to meet him in an hour, and I don't have anything to wear to a symphony so we need to hurry this counseling session along."

"Max, honey, it's nine a.m. on a Saturday morning. You're probably not going to the symphony, and even if you were, this guy should have the decency and common sense to tell you that in advance."

This was probably true. Jory was all about common sense.

"Call him," she said. "Ask for the dress code if you don't want to pump him for all the details. If he's a *good* guy, he'll be able to give you that much. If he can't, perhaps this romantic opportunity is one you should reevaluate." She moved toward the staircase. "I have to finish making snacks for all of our soccer games. I know you can handle this."

Mallori marched up the stairs and closed the door with a definitive thud that made clear her expectation I was dating someone less horrible and emotionally ruinous than Teddy.

Since Jory was none of those things and I was out of time to ponder my clothing options, I snatched up my phone and tapped Jory's number. All I had to do was ask about the dress code. One quick question. This was fine. No problem. I could pull this off without being a tool.

"Hey," he answered, a little breathless as if he'd dashed to grab his phone. "What's up?"

Or—oh, Jesus, no—he was breathless because he hated talking on the phone and this was causing him distress. Oh my god. I was torturing this poor man. I should've just gone with the suit I wore to my Uncle Grover's funeral ten years ago and suffered the consequences. No amount of inappropriate attire was worth stressing Jory.

I dragged a hand down my face. I had to say something. I couldn't just hang up. We were doing this, we were having a phone conversation and I was going to dissolve into a hard ball of my bad choices any minute now. "Would it be okay—I mean, do you mind—where are we going?"

So much for one quick question.

"Oh," Jory replied, laughing. "Yeah, of course. We're—"

"Here's the thing," I interrupted because I couldn't stop the words from tumbling out. This was already bad. Why not make it worse? "I don't have anything to wear to the symphony, and I don't really know what a symposium is or whether it's at all related to a symphony—though I figure it has to be, right? No? Anyway, I'm not sure what to wear to a symphony. Or a symposium. And I don't want to screw this up again—or any more than I am right now with all this word salad. So, if I haven't convinced you I'm a raving lunatic yet, I'd love to know where we're going."

Jory laughed again. "Wow. Okay."

I thumped my forehead against the wall. "Yep. I've screwed it up again."

"You haven't screwed up anything," Jory replied. "I should've given you more info yesterday. It's my fault."

"Not your fault," I insisted. "Really, it's just me over-thinking. You probably would've said something about needing a tux since you're always hot on the details like that."

"You definitely won't need a tux for the day I have planned," he said. "I thought it would be fun to do the pumpkin patch thing."

"A pumpkin patch?"

"Yeah. I found a big farm in the area with all the usual farm stuff on Instagram. I know it's the most basic thing ever but it's a mandatory autumn activity, right? I also want an excuse to eat some fresh apple cider donuts. Does that work for you?" When I didn't respond right away, Jory added, "We can do something else. It doesn't have to be a pumpkin patch."

I glanced at the navy sweater, the one that practically screamed *autumn in New England,* and I let out an enormous sigh of relief. "That sounds awesome."

"So…do you still want me to pick you up in an hour?"

"Hell yeah," I replied. "I'll be out on the curb doing jumping jacks."

"I look forward to seeing that," Jory said with a laugh. "Hey, Max?"

"Yeah?"

"Have you been tearing your closet apart and pacing in your underwear?"

I jerked a shoulder up. "Basically."

After a pause, he said, "Me too."

"But—why? You know where we're going."

He paused again. "Because I don't want to screw this up either."

The back of my neck heated, then my cheeks. And I was smiling, not that Jory could see any of it but maybe he was feeling this way too. Maybe we were both blushing and tender and scared as hell to get this wrong because we knew it could be very, very right.

"And there's something else I should say," he added. "I want to apologize."

"You can't dump me right now. Not when we've established I'm going a little nutty and pacing in my underwear."

"No, that's not what I'm saying," Jory replied with a stiff laugh. "I feel bad that it's taken me so long to warm up. Sometimes, I experience changes like new jobs, new cities, new homes—"

"New guys," I added.

"New guys, yes," he agreed. "I experience some of that change as little traumas. Even if it's a good change, a wonderful change, my system needs extra time to regain homeostasis. It's like I can't do anything until I've accepted those changes, integrated them into my operating system, and found that new normal because my brain and body are in survival mode. That's why it took me so long to go out with you in the first place and why I'm still on eggshells."

"You don't have to apologize," I said. "I know you're just processing. I can tell. I see it. It's like you're thinking real hard to solve a problem."

"You're being extremely tolerant. I know you'd like it if I just hurried up and—"

"No," I interrupted. "Actually, no. Expecting you to

hurry up because I'm kind of obsessed with you is a quick way to send you running for the hills. I don't want that for me, and I also don't want to be the guy who scared off everyone's new favorite science teacher."

"So, you've thought about this," Jory said.

I could picture him arching his eyebrow up and giving me a sharp look. Loved it.

"Sure have," I replied. "I know I'd rather respect your needs and make you feel safe than anything else. I like you, Hayzer. I plan on hanging around as long as you'll have me."

"But..." He laughed, but it was the kind of noise that came without humor, without light. "But why?"

I was *this close* to detailing the frequency with which I eye-fucked him but stopped myself and replayed that humorless laugh. "Do you need compliments, or do you need me to explain why you're worthy of affection?"

"I need—" he started, all crisp and snappy with his tone "—well, I guess I need to understand why you'd put up with all this from me. It's a lot to ask. Most people can't handle it."

Though he couldn't see it, I curled my arm into a bicep flex. "Most people aren't Coach Maximum."

"Why do I get the impression you're flexing something right now?"

"Because you're a fan of my fire power," I replied. "You also care about things in big, deep ways. You think more than anyone else I know and you listen even more. When you talk, people pay attention because you're thoughtful and informed. I figure you're one of the good ones. You're worth my patience. Plus, you're hot as fuck and kiss like a porn star."

"Max," he said, my name barely a sigh. "You're making me rethink this pumpkin patch idea."

I fisted my hand in my hair as a chill washed over my bare chest, down my spine. "Oh. Okay then. Um...I'm sorry."

"Oh, shit. No, not—I mean—if my roommate didn't make such a big deal about his no-visitors policy, we could just hang out here. Or we could get some pumpkins and then come back here and...and see what happens."

I pulled the phone away from my ear, frowned at it a moment before asking, "Are you saying we'd have naked bedroom time if it weren't for your roommate?"

"I'm saying I like you too," he replied. "I'll see you in an hour for the pumpkin farm. Okay?"

"Yeah, okay." A strangled groan rattled in my throat. "Look, I have to deal with my dick's interest in naked bedroom time—"

"Yours too?"

I pressed my forehead to the wall. "Jory. Babe. Sweetheart. You can't say that unless you plan on letting me listen while you jerk it."

There was a pause, and then, "I wouldn't mind that. If I can listen to you."

Above me, my sister yelled for her kids to gather their soccer equipment. Her husband yelled back something about a phone charger. The kids yelled about missing cleats, missing hoodies, missing shin guards. Feet pounded down the stairs, across the first floor. All while my dick throbbed against my belly.

We couldn't do this. Not right now. Not with all...*that*. I couldn't focus with the kids hollering at each other and my brother-in-law counting down the seconds they had to get their shit together. I couldn't perform under these conditions.

"Just imagine I'm there," Jory continued. "And I pull your underwear down. That's what you want, isn't it?"

"*Ohmygodyes*," I groaned. My boxers hit the floor.

"Then I stroke you," he went on. I didn't know where the fuck Dirty Jory came from but I was all about this side of him. "You like it when I slowly twist my fist from the base all the way over your head, don't you?"

I shuttled my hand over my cock while my brother-in-law shouted, "I will only count down from ten one more time."

"That's right," Jory said. "And you like it when I give it to you fast. It isn't pretty like this, with me stroking you so hard that all you can do is take it. You give me that beautiful groan, the one that tells me you need this so badly. The one that says you'd come on the spot if I sucked you for even a minute."

My sister stomped her foot overhead, saying, "This is your last chance to get in the car. If you're not ready to go, we're skipping the game."

"No games today," my brother-in-law yelled.

"You need this so badly, baby," Jory repeated.

His voice was thick and breathless, but not the same kind of breathless as when he answered the phone. This was a hot and sweaty form of breathless, the kind that came from—oh, *fuuuuuck*, if I listened closely, I could hear him jerking himself. The slide of skin over skin, a grunt, a hitch in his breathing.

"Yes," I whispered, my hand moving over my shaft faster, *faster*. "I'm—I want—*with you*."

"I'm there, baby, I'm there," he said, his voice pitching up and shattering the words into small, panting syllables. A deep, satisfied grunt followed and that was it for me, that was all I needed to spill into my hand, down my leg, onto my foot and the floor. "That's right. Give me everything, baby. Keep going. Let me have it."

A minute passed as my strokes slowed and the last spurts of my orgasm flooded my hand. My heart was thumping in my chest, my breath coming in ragged exhales, and I couldn't hear anything but the tender caress of Jory's words in my ear.

Eventually, I said, "Hey, Jory?"

"Yeah, Max?"

"That was...well, I don't know what to say other than holy fuckballs."

"That's all right. Holy fuckballs works for me," he replied.

"Okay good. But, listen. I gotta rinse off now if you're showing up here in"—I blinked at the clock—"forty-five minutes. I don't even know what I'm wearing yet."

"Yeah, same," he said with a laugh.

"I'd rather shower with you," I added.

"Yeah, same," he repeated. "I'll see you soon, Max."

I PICKED my way down a quiet lane of not-quite-ripe pumpkins with Jory at my side. The sun was high and bright, the air cool and crisp, and I hadn't thought about what I was wearing since Jory had greeted me with an unexpectedly hot kiss. Maybe I should've expected it after that phone call. Maybe I'd read Jory all wrong. A person could be anxious and introverted while also being boldly sexual. All of these things could be true at once.

"This looks like a good place to sit down," he said, gesturing to a clear spot ahead.

We settled on the grass and spread out our coffees and bag of hot donuts. If today was an indication of Jory's speed, I wasn't going to complain. It suited me just fine.

"This is nice," Jory said, handing me half a donut. "I like being able to talk to you. Our schedules are so different at school that I hardly see you."

"And we were too busy sprinting from one leg of the first date race to another last weekend to make much conversation," I quipped.

He elbowed me in the ribs. "How many times do I have to tell you I had fun? I was exhausted and still can't get that weird stain out of my shirt but it was an epic first date."

I shoved my portion of the donut in my mouth to stop myself from apologizing—again. After a swig of coffee, I asked, "I know why I'm worried about messing every-thing up but why are you?"

Jory busied himself with inspecting the rest of the

cinnamon-sugared donuts. He didn't meet my gaze when he said, "I generally worry about messing up all things."

"But—why? You're smart and cute and"—I gave his slim cut jeans, plaid shirt, and quilted vest a plainly appreciative glance—"you look like a hot L.L. Bean catalog."

"And you look like a hot Under Armour catalog." He shifted, reaching for his back pocket. "Here. Let's get a pic. I'm aiming for full-on basic today. That, and I want to remember the day I got to rub up against you and snuggle in the dirt."

"First of all, you have a standing invitation to snuggle me in the dirt or anywhere at all," I replied. "And second, let me get that cinnamon-sugar mustache you're rocking since I know you're not going to want that in your pics." I leaned in, kissed the sweetness right off him. I wanted to press him down, lay my body over his, and show him what it really meant to rub up against me. But there were pumpkins everywhere, not to mention people, and Jory wanted his Instagrammable moment. "Much better."

"Yeah? You got it all? You didn't miss any?" he teased, a smile tipping up the corners of his mouth. "Maybe you should check one more time."

"You're right. More thorough attention is required." I lifted my hand to cup his clean-shaven jaw and brushed my lips over his. He edged closer and I took that as an invitation to drag him into my lap. I lashed my arm around his waist, settled his legs over my thigh, and tugged him tight against my chest. "You're going to have grass stains on your jeans," I murmured. "Dirt too."

"Should probably take them off right away." I could feel the smile in his kiss. "Gotta treat those stains properly or they'll set in."

I closed my fingers around the back of his vest, caught his bottom lip between my teeth, groaned at the twist of need in my belly. "I have no clue whether we like these stains or not, Jory," I rumbled. "I just know I want to get your pants off as soon as you'll let me."

He twined his arms around my neck and shoved his fingers through my hair. Everything about him felt unbelievably good. His body was tight and lean, he smelled like expensive herbs, and his lips destroyed me.

Eventually, he leaned back, tidied my hair, and said, "I'm serious about getting that perfect autumn photo."

I smoothed a hand down my chest to straighten the sweater he'd rucked up. "I'm serious about getting you naked, but I won't cry about being your arm candy if that's what you want."

"It is," he replied with a cheeky grin.

Out of absolutely nowhere, a woman with one of those fancy professional cameras around her neck appeared. She pointed at the phone Jory held up, asking, "Do you want me to take that for you? You don't really want it to look like a selfie, do you?"

"Of course not," Jory replied, handing her the phone. "Thank you."

She backed up a step and focused on the screen. I squeezed his waist. He nipped at my jaw. "I'm so glad we're not at the symphony," I said under my breath.

"Because there are no wandering photographers at the

symphony?" he asked, that warm laughter ripe in his words.

"Because the only suit I have would never conceal the boner your cinnamon-sugar mustache caused."

"I caused?" Jory ran his knuckles over my scruffy chin. "I believe it was a group effort."

"Big smiles," she said. "Say *pumpkins*!"

We didn't say *pumpkins* but we did laugh, and I knew the image would be a keeper. I knew Jory was a keeper.

When she handed Jory's phone back to him, she said to me, "I can take one for you too."

Before I could argue about Jory simply sharing his pic with me, I retrieved my device and swiped open the camera app. "That would be great."

"All right, this time you're saying *pumpkins* or I'm giving you two the mom stare," she said.

"I know that look. My sister is a pro at the mom stare," I said. "But I have to warn you. We might have you beat with teacher stares."

"Bring it on," she said. "Now, say *pumpkins*!"

We complied this time, and she made an amused face at the screen. "That came out goofier than anything my twins have ever managed. Well done."

"Hear that?" I asked Jory. "We're extra goofy."

"It's a good complement to extra hard," he replied under his breath.

I kissed the sharp line of his cheekbone as she murmured, "Awww." Then, with a hand over her forehead to block out the sun as she peered at the screen, "Oh. Oh, that's a sweet one. It's just precious."

The woman returned my phone and dug a business card out of her shoulder bag. "I do a little photography work. Mostly maternity and newborn stuff but I like getting to work with couples too. It brings me joy to work with people who can't get enough of each other. Babies are the best but so are people who are clearly in mad, crazy love. Hit me up when you're ready for an engagement shoot."

Jory's lips parted as her words registered. "Thanks. We'll keep that in mind."

I accepted the card because I didn't want to leave the nice lady hanging but it was safe to say engagement photos were one of the last things on my mind. Even if we jerked off together this morning, this was our *second* date. It'd taken Jory a month to agree to the first one. Even from the most optimistic view, engagement photos were miles and miles away.

And I tucked that card in my wallet just the same.

"That was interesting," he murmured as she retreated. "You know, for a sales pitch."

I shrugged. "I think we're pretty adorable."

"Shut your mouth. Of course, we're adorable." He smiled as he swatted my chest. "That's why it looks like we're in mad, crazy love."

"In that case, maybe we should take a break from expecting to fuck this all up. I'd say we make a good team, Hayzer." I handed him another donut and grabbed one for myself. "What d'you say?"

"I reserve the right to worry irrationally at any time," he replied, his focus trained on the donut. "It's part of my charm."

Since my arm was still locked around Jory's waist, I had to station my donut on the lid of my coffee and pray I didn't create chaos with that maneuver. "Does that make my hella nasty breakup with a serial cheater last year part of my charm? Because it's one hundred percent of the reason why I tried to impress you with the best date in the history of dates last weekend and had a low-key panic attack over sweaters this morning."

"Don't forget the bit about the symphony," he added. "Because that was totally part of it too."

"Thanks for the reminder."

After an easy smile, Jory asked, "What's the story with this ex?"

I didn't want to rehash the epic tragedy of Teddy and me but I'd brought it up, and sooner or later, I was going to have to share this part of myself with Jory. It was much like divulging sexual health histories and exchanging notes on food allergies—boring, occasionally gross, but necessary if we wanted to be on the same wavelength. Or naked.

With a gusty sigh, I said, "On and off for two years. Then, lived together for three years. Cheated on me from the very beginning."

"Oh, shit."

Yeah. That was the usual response.

"Pretty much," I replied. "I moved out and ended things last winter. That's how I landed at my sister's house. I only have to babysit her kids about once a week when she and her husband have their date nights as payment. That and letting her spray me down with all her therapist juju. It could be worse."

Jory ignored all my quippy comments and drilled into the heart of the matter. "How are you doing?"

"I'm good," I admitted, and I meant it. "I'm still in my head a bit because anyone who is cheated on for years assumes they did something to cause it, they did something to attract someone who uses and abuses people. But I've had nearly a full year to be sad and angry, and then sad some more. I've gone through down phases and dark phases, and some ragey, bitter ones too. At some point, I stopped having feelings about the breakup and how everything went down with us, and all the garbage feelings started drifting away."

I passed my coffee to my other hand and knuckled some sugar from his upper lip because it was there but also because I wanted to touch him again. Wanted to laugh with him and hold him close, just like this, and keep my old dramas in the past.

"Are they completely gone? The garbage feelings?" he added.

"Well, I met this blindingly hot guy when he was on campus for new staff orientation—"

"Blindingly hot, huh?" Jory asked with a smirk.

"In fact, the only thing I could see was this guy with good hair and marine life on his ties. After that, I didn't think about the ex too often. I freaked out about dumb stuff like what to wear and whether I'd blown it the first time we got together, and those are total garbage feelings but they're different. It's different. I'm relearning how to take care of myself. My sister has other words for it but I think that's the main idea, you know?"

"I do know." Jory studied me for a long moment, long enough to make me wonder whether I'd said too much, shared too deep. Then, "Maybe it is part of your charm. It's okay if our charm gets a little banged up along the way, don't you think? Or a lot banged up. I just—I have to believe we're all good and worthy even when we don't have clear, concise stories where everything we went through makes sense, and our issues are predictable and our quirks are only minorly quirky, never distractingly quirky. Sometimes big, shitty things happen like a serial cheater and it makes us twitchy about new relationships. Other times, we have a slightly chaotic childhood and we're almost paralyzed with anxiety as adults. The hit doesn't have to be hard to leave a dent. And regardless of the size of that dent, I need to believe we're all okay. That it's our rusty, banged up charm calling out and asking for acceptance."

I wasn't in mad, crazy love with Jory.

Though I wasn't nearly as far away from it as I'd originally thought.

PART III

WINTER

5

JORY

THERE WAS a gravity tied to each school year, a forward motion with a speed dictated by the combination of my teaching assignment, the mix of students in my classes, my colleagues, and my reactions to all those things.

Certain years crawled by, each day passing more glacially than the previous. Others were there and done before I knew it. The problem was, I rarely knew which one I was in at the time. Teaching railroaded you like that. Exhausted you like that. It was a three-foot job that required thirty-thousand-foot planning, and it was nearly impossible to know how it was going until stepping far outside it.

This was only one of the reasons I looked forward to the winter holiday break each year. By that point, I was in desperate need of time off to recover from exams, the end of the grading period, and all the special seasonal events. I never did any holiday shopping until after school was out for break because getting through it all was the best I could manage.

I was incredibly fortunate to be dating a man who not only understood these things about me but shared some degree of my late December frenzy. Max didn't give big exams and his end-of-term grades were much less complicated but he still had his hands full. Whereas I taught three grade levels, Max taught *nine*. He had to turn in a grade for every single kid, kindergarten through eighth grade. Despite that load, he was helping me grade my exams.

"Aren't you two the cutest?" Mallori cooed as she walked into the kitchen. "It's like you're doing homework together."

"Except it's not homework and we're trying to get this done so we can drink gin and tonics all night," Max replied, an orange pen cap jammed between his teeth as he scanned the paper in front of him.

"Don't forget the white elephant," I added. "Or, as you put it, *the weirdest gift wins* swap."

We were headed to a holiday party with Max's friend group tonight. I'd met his crew several times in the past couple of months and they were a great bunch though they were a bit leery of me. More, they were leery of anyone hurting their friend again. That was the story I told myself because stepping into any situation where people held me at a distance and shot well-intentioned warning glances in my direction turned my anxiety up to ninety-five.

It was a good thing they were fun and Max never left

me alone for more than a bathroom break because their desire to pounce was palpable. I wasn't positive but I had the sneaking suspicion they'd run a background check on me too. There was no other way they could've known I'd worked at an ice cream shop—same as Max I'd discovered—in high school.

"Right. Can't skip that," Max said. "But go ahead with your happy homemaker fantasies, Mal. We won't stop you."

"It's not my happy homemaker fantasy." She scoffed as she folded a kitchen towel, wiped the countertop, and folded it again. "I just like having you guys here."

"You're a lot like my sister," I said, smiling at Mallori. "You and Keaton are totally different beings but she likes to have family around. Something about people being together pleases her."

Mallori shook out the towel and folded it again. "Well, I'd love to meet her. Your mom too. We could have a get-together sometime."

Max glanced up from the exam in front of him, shrugged. "What would happen if our sisters hit it off? What if they teamed up?"

"That would be an exciting event," I replied. "Your sister, the marriage counselor. My sister, the divorce attorney. They could launch a referral program."

Mallori rolled her eyes and gave us an on-point, mom-branded *pshahh* before opening the refrigerator. "You're sure you're not hungry? You don't want anything to eat before you go?"

"We'll eat there," Max replied, running his finger down the line of multiple choice answers.

"Will you actually eat or will you nibble then come home famished and raid my cupboards at two in the morning?"

"I'll eat," Max said. "Jory will nibble off my plate. We'll still raid the cupboards."

"That's probably true," I added. "We might also order a pizza but we'll be quiet about it."

Mallori laughed into the fridge. "I love you guys."

"And we love you," he replied.

"You'll get a ride home, right? You're not driving to this party?" she asked.

"We aren't driving," Max assured her.

"And you'll stay the night, Jory?" She turned her concerned gaze on me. "I don't want you out on the roads too late."

I wasn't totally comfortable staying at Mallori's house. It wasn't about her or her family so much as I wasn't comfortable in anyone's house. But tonight was an exception. We were going to a party that didn't start until eight o'clock, and we were *this* close to the winter holidays, and we needed to blow off some steam. At this point, my anxiety was taking a back seat to my screeching need to get thoroughly laid.

Thank god we were heading up to the mountains the day after Christmas. We'd snagged a cute little Airbnb on the slopes at Sugarloaf as our gift to each other. Seven full days *alone* in a cabin with Max was the best gift ever.

To this point, we'd only managed moments of intimacy. A phone call, an evening in his garden apartment (which sounded so much better than *the basement)*, a night together when my roommate wasn't around to complain. It was great—better than great. The sex was *amazing*. But I needed a lot more than moments here, one-off nights there.

"Yeah. I'll stay," I said to her. Not wanting to press the issue any further, I turned to Max. "What did you end up grabbing for the white elephant? I forgot to thank you for doing that."

"Don't mention it." He shook his head. "It gave me a chance to get a little engagement gift for Tom and Wes. For the weirdest gift competition, I got a birdhouse shingled in flattened beer cans and a package of rose chocolate truffles decorated to look like breasts."

"Oh, Max," Mallori said with a sigh. "I'll leave you to it. Have fun tonight, boys."

"We will," he called as she wandered into the living room. He held up an exam, saying to me, "Vrenda fell apart on the second half. Like, completely lost her momentum."

"I was worried about that." I took the exam from him and skimmed the incorrect responses. "She gets in her head. I've worked on it with her but if she comes across a question she's not sure about, she doubts everything from that point forward." I frowned at the page. Every single one was wrong. "I'll have her retake this section during lunch next week. She knows this stuff."

"I like that we allow do-overs," Max said as he moved to another exam. "When you think about it, very few adults have jobs where they only get one chance to do it right. Even then, it's after years of practice. Surgeons go to school for ages before they're left alone to operate on hearts. Pilots have to log tons of hours before they get their license. It doesn't make sense that we expect kids to nail it in one shot and that's the end of the chances."

I nodded in agreement. "I wish I'd been able to retake exams when I was a kid. It would've preserved some shred of my sanity. All I did was worry about one test or another." I shook my head and moved another paper to the top of my stack. "I tried to walk the sixth graders through some in-the-moment coping strategies last week because they were a hot, messy mess during my review session."

"The first round of term-end assessments always freaks them out," Max said. "They go from the calm, loving embrace of Audrey's fifth grade to this middle school hellscape where they have different teachers, different classrooms, a different bell schedule, *and* summative exams." He straightened his stack and tucked them into the Brattle Book Shop canvas tote I used for graded papers. The NPR tote held the ungraded ones. The NPR tote was rarely empty. "But they have you to help them through those growing pains even if Avila goes and scares the shit out of them in the math block."

"Isn't that the truth."

My colleagues were incredible. The best of the best. Juliana Avila, the math instructor, was as tough as nails. What I offered our students in grounding techniques, she met with stone-faced, no-nonsense, and high expectations. She loved the kids, and she loved the work, but it looked different on her than it did on me. Neither of us was right or wrong. Teaching styles and demeanors varied, and that was a good thing. Kids needed all different kinds of role models and connection points. A fine example of that came in my colleagues in the English and history departments.

Clark Kerrin and Noa Elbaz argued about everything but they did it in a painfully polite way that cut and sliced until they were nothing more than finely shredded echoes of people. And somehow, they did this while making the students think it was a funny little game, a rivalry of sorts, like cross-town high school football teams. I had to believe they had styles independent of this ongoing rivalry, but I couldn't imagine them without each other.

"Are you almost ready to pack this up?" Max asked. "We can finish the rest tomorrow."

"I have to grade lab reports tomorrow," I replied as I counted up the incorrect responses and scribbled that number at the bottom of the page. "Give me five minutes. I'll get these done."

Max reached across the table. "Give me a few more. We'll do this together."

———

MAX'S FRIENDS Tom and Wes hosted tonight's gathering in their South End brownstone. We'd been here once before for game night and the place was decorated like a chic magazine spread, all one-of-a-kind pieces mixed with modern glam and earthy neutrals.

It was the perfect fit for them, though, to be fair, I didn't know Wes at all. I'd met him at the game night event but we'd sat with different groups on opposite sides of the apartment and shared little more than polite greetings and goodbyes. Tom, however, I'd grown friendly with in recent weeks. We had a bit in common and picked up each other's vibe right away. Our tendencies ran toward nerdy, high strung, and bespectacled with funky ties. Others saw us as remote or closed off, we worked a lot more than was healthy, and we were attached to large, gregarious men.

Tom and Wes got engaged over the summer and were still in the date-setting phase. Last I'd heard from Tom, Wes's business travel schedule had kept him on the go in recent months, but they were hoping to make some decisions over the holidays.

Tom worked on the finance and holdings side of an architecture firm. I didn't have a full accounting of the facts, and Tom was particularly tight-lipped on the matter, but as best I could gather, Wes trained private military and spy forces for a living. I couldn't say I'd ever met someone in that profession before.

Max's friends were as important to him as his family and our colleagues. There was no future for us if I couldn't get one of these guys on my side, and I was thankful he counted a quiet, bookish boy like Tom among his favorite people.

A bright, true grin split my face when the door swept

open and I saw Tom on the other side. "You made it," he shouted over the noise behind him. "Come here, come here." He held his arms wide and closed us into a crushing group hug. "So happy you're here."

"You make it sound like you haven't seen us in a decade. Pretty sure it hasn't been more than two weeks." Max pressed a bottle of champagne into Tom's hand. "Happy holidays, young man."

Tom held the bottle out to study the label. "You shouldn't have," he yelped. "What are you doing, bringing the good bubbles into my house. Are you trying to get me naked, Murphy?"

From literal thin air, Wes appeared, his blond brows arching down as he asked, "What was that?"

Tom angled the champagne toward his fiancé. "Max and Jory brought the good stuff."

"I never did get you an engagement gift," Max said with a shrug.

It was curious how he made it seem as though his gestures weren't deliberate. Almost like it was better—simpler, perhaps—to be the lovable goofball instead of the thoughtful, intentional man.

Wes hooked a beefy arm around Max's neck and pulled him in for a hug that looked more like wrestling than an embrace. Tom eyed them for a moment before reaching out and squeezing my forearm.

"So good to see you. And I can't get over that tie." He tapped the knot at my throat, grinning at the dark green fabric embroidered with blazing red poinsettias. "Where do you find these things? I need to know so I can steal your style."

"I wish I could tell you," I said as Max and Wes shifted out into the exterior hallway and fell deep into conversation. "They were my grandfather's. All of my ties were his."

Tom studied the knot again. "He's a selfless man to part with such a sharp collection."

I shook my head. "When he passed away a few years ago, my mom asked me to go through his things and take anything I wanted before she donated it all. He was a bigger guy, so I doubt she expected me to touch the clothes. She thought I'd want books, old news clippings, random stuff. Mementos, you know?"

He nodded and edged closer to hear me over the music and conversation. Parties were the worst places to talk but people were always hell-bent on doing it anyway. "Of course," he said. "I'm so sorry for your loss. Were you close?"

"Not when I was a kid but more toward the end." I ran a hand down my chest, feeling the outline of the tie under my sweater. "I visited him on the weekends. His home health aides only came for an hour on Saturdays and Sundays, so he was mostly on his own. My mom needed help because she couldn't afford the extra coverage and it wasn't like he'd let a babysitter come in to make his lunch or fix the television when it blitzed out. So, I'd drive up from college and watch football games with him. I'm not a huge football fan but that wasn't the point. I got to know him. The person, not the grandfather. I hadn't realized until then he had an existence completely separate from my experiences with him. That everyone has experiences completely separate from the role they play in your life." I traced the outline of the tie again. "He didn't really need me to stay the whole day. He fell asleep before the first half of every game."

"And now you have all his swanky ties as a reminder of that man and his existence," Tom said. "I love that story."

I bobbed my head in agreement. It wasn't like me to reveal so many truths at once, though there was something gentle and accepting about Tom, like he knew how to draw out and care for even the most broken and battered among us.

"I'm happy you're here," he said with a quick glance at Max and Wes in the hall. "You're good for him. I like the look of you two together."

I had an effusive response at the ready, some "that's so kind of you to say" and "thank you for having me" and a bit of "your home is lovely" and a final dash of "merry everything" but another of Max's friends swooped in, effectively bursting that gentle, accepting bubble Tom had built around us.

"Hello, hello," Pawl sang, looping his elbow with mine. His long, dark hair hung loose around his shoulders tonight and he wore a headband embellished with a small, glittering Santa hat. It was gorgeous against his porcelain skin. Pawl was a corporate attorney by day but that didn't interfere with his headband collection or the skirts he paired with his suit coats and ties. "It's a delight to see your gorgeous face again, Jory. Come along, let's get you a drink. It's the holidays after all. Must be jolly."

I gave Tom *save me* eyes, but Pawl caught his elbow too. "Oh—but—we were just—"

"Let's leave the daddies to talk," Pawl interrupted with a wink in Wes and Max's direction. "It's important business, being beastly and all. They're probably comparing their body-hair grooming routines and comparing beard oil products. Very important business. They'll know where to find you when they've exhausted those topics or they realize they haven't pawed at you in five minutes. Whichever comes first."

Pawl led us into the white marble kitchen and started mixing several cocktails while Tom restocked the charcuterie board. In the time it took Pawl to rub a lime wedge around the rims of five highball glasses, the group swelled to include Joseph, Flinn, and Bryce.

I'd only met Bryce once before this evening and it'd been shortly after his mother's death. At the time, he'd barely managed a weary smile, a handshake, and a promise that he was usually much more fun. He was dark skinned, slim, and very tall, the version of tall that required him to duck when walking through most doorways. He practiced law at the same firm as Pawl.

Joseph, Pawl's partner, was a wide-shouldered dental hygienist who routinely asked me which part of Vermont I was from and whether I was vegan. I couldn't tell if the Vermont thing was a passive-aggressive move or I wasn't adequately memorable to make all my previous responses stick. I refused to believe he'd forgotten.

Flinn worked in pro sports publicity, always seemed genuinely interested in talking about whichever science topic was in the news that week, and was currently in a relationship with a woman. I wasn't sure whether he was pan or bi and didn't know him well enough to open that conversation.

Save for Max and Wes, who now seemed strategically absent, the core of Max's friend group was all here. Gathered around me.

My stomach dropped. Oh, hell. Fuck. This was an ambush. An interrogation with liquor and fancy cheeses as implements. *Fuck.* They'd planned this. Oh my god, they'd *planned* this. I gulped down a breath of sand and scrap metal.

Pawl handed me a drink and motioned for everyone to join him in raising their glasses. "To new friends," he drawled. "And old ones too. It's not like I'm going anywhere."

"I'd like to see you try to get rid of me," Flinn said to the clinking of glasses.

The group shifted after the toast, and Bryce and Pawl positioned themselves on either side of me while Joseph, Tom, and Flinn brought the circle in close. The six of us were tucked into a narrow space between the kitchen island and the refrigerator. By all accounts, this wasn't a great situation for me since I was the only one who didn't know what was happening.

I locked both hands around my glass, thankful for the cool dampness of the condensation as the back of my neck flamed.

"So, Jory, we're hoping you could clue us in on a few things." Pawl sent a meaningful glance to the other members of the ambush squad. Sweat rolled down my spine and soaked my shirt. "If you don't mind."

I took a sip of my drink, something limey with a confident pour of vodka, to buy myself a minute. I did this whenever I needed a pause from my students—save for the vodka. It gave me time to think and breathe. There were moments when I had to tamp down some frustration or conceal a laugh in my water bottle. Kids often said hilarious and wildly inappropriate things. Even the best of us struggled to keep a straight face sometimes.

I wasn't sure I could keep a straight face for this. I kept my gaze on a tight circuit between the door—*come on, Max, get in here*—and my interrogators. Still, I didn't know what I'd do if they'd staged this coup to break up Max and me. Would they do that? *Could* they? I didn't need their approval but contending with their disapproval was a different story. And why would they disapprove? I had more than my share of issues but that didn't mean I needed to be run out of town.

Pawl draped his arm over my shoulders, leaning in close to ask, "How is he doing? We're worried about him."

"I—what?" I blinked at him, thoroughly confused.

"He looks so much better," Joseph offered. "He looks alive again."

"Happy too," Bryce added. "You can tell his spirit is in a much better place."

"How is he doing?" Pawl repeated. "Have you noticed any Eeyore days?"

I shook my head. "I have no idea what you're talking about."

Tom nodded, finally understanding my confusion. "After Max left his ex, he went through some difficult periods. Some Eeyore days. You know Eeyore. From *Winnie the Pooh*. He used to be all Tigger but things went from bad to worse with Teddy. Tigger faded away. Eeyore took over."

"I don't believe that," I said with a shocked, humorless laugh. I knew he'd struggled after his breakup but this sounded nothing like the Max I knew. "I can't see Max being—being Eeyore."

Bryce and Flinn exchanged a loaded glance. "Believe me," Flinn said. "It was a rough time for him. It seemed like he was slipping into a depression, but he didn't want to discuss it with any of us."

"He never wants to bother anyone," Bryce added. "Even when we want to be bothered."

"Especially then," Joseph said.

"We didn't know what to expect when he told us he'd met someone." Tom tipped his chin in my direction. I was the *someone*. "We were worried it wouldn't be healthy for him."

"Thanks," I muttered.

"You are adorable and all the precious things," Joseph said. "But we didn't know that at the start. We didn't know if it was a rebound or a repeat of the cycle with Teddy—"

"I don't cheat on people," I said, louder than I'd antici-pated by the sudden snap of quiet.

"Of course not," Tom said.

"Dude, we're Team Max, and you're the MVP of that team," Flinn said. "We're asking you these questions because we want to believe he's out of the Eeyore days, but since he's spending all his free time with you, we're not sure what's up or down."

When I didn't respond because I was honestly trying to put all of this information into a logical order while also convincing my brain this wasn't a fight-or-flight situation, Bryce said, "We need to know if he's really doing okay or if we should push him to visit a doctor for some help. I'd been keeping an eye on the situation, but then my mom passed, and my entire life was on hold for three months."

"And I had to duck out when a few of my athletes got caught up in a gambling scandal," Flinn said. "I've spent the past couple of months on the road more than off and I didn't check in with Max nearly enough."

"I got engaged," Tom said, holding up his hand to show off his ring. "And we left town for a bunch of weddings and then we spent a month hiking overseas. I know I didn't talk to him nearly enough."

"We've been shitty friends," Pawl said. "That's what we're trying to tell you. Max would run barefoot through the streets if we needed him, and somehow, we all managed to flake out on him when he needed us too much to ask for it." He shook his head and glanced down at the floor, his lips pressed together in a line as his chin wobbled. "We had the situation with Max and his Eeyore moments in hand until life cocked it up for us this summer. Now that we're not falling apart anymore, we want to thank you for being there for him. He's happy as a fucking clam and we're damn lucky he found you. He can't stop talking about you, by the way, so please don't break his heart." He tapped his glass to mine. "We've probably been shitty friends to you too, but I swear to gumdrops, we're working on it. Now, tell us. How's Coach doing?"

I parted my lips to respond but Max's blond head and smiling face joined the group. "There you are, babe!" He pushed his way through the wall of my finely dressed captors, cupped my jaw, and kissed me as if we'd been separated for years rather than minutes. When he came up for air, he plucked the cocktail from my hands and swallowed it in two gulps. He held up the empty glass, saying, "Another, please. My boy has worked his ass off this week and he deserves some holiday cheer. Move it, Joey. I know you can mix a cocktail faster than that."

I caught Tom's eye and grinned. "All Tigger."

AS PREDICTED, we didn't get back to Mallori's house until late. After midnight, before dawn. Somewhere in the middle. The specifics of it were hazed over and gilded around the edges as only vodka could. Vodka and fiercely protective friends.

Since Tom and Wes sent us home with a holiday-printed Pyrex dish of leftovers—which we gorged in the back of the Uber to some extremely righteous Christian rock—we didn't raid Mallori's kitchen or call up for pizza.

Instead, we stumbled into the house, laughing and groping and loudly shushing each other as we shrugged out of our coats, kicked off our shoes. The now-empty Pyrex found its way to the sink with a clatter that probably woke the entire street. Max gathered me up in an embrace that was more tackle than hug and flattened a hand over my mouth.

"You're in my bed tonight," he said, wedging his thigh between my legs. "I want you there every fuckin' night, Jory. You know that?"

It wasn't a question in search of a response but I nodded anyway. I did know. He told me this almost once a week. On occasion, he shared this along with visual proof. His cock in gym shorts or boxer briefs. Under a thin sheet or in his fist. Dripping wet after a shower. I *knew*.

Neither of us was in a situation where we could manage regular sleepovers. My roommate was nuts about keeping everything just so and he hated unscheduled visitors. Max lived here with a family of four and often had unscheduled visitors in the form of his niece or nephew bounding down the basement stairs to tell him some amazing new thing.

None of these conditions were ripe for the carnality of a hot new relationship.

We spent a lot of time kissing in cars. We took long walks, went to the movies, ate at cozy restaurants where it was *necessary* to sit extremely close together rather than a product of our lust. And we capped those outings with at least an hour of car kissing. On the nights we retreated to Max's place, we'd settle a blanket over our laps and ignore the television while maintaining some deniability if the kids—or Mallori—came down for a visit.

And still, it wasn't enough.

"Downstairs," Max growled into my ear. "I want you downstairs *now*."

He led the way, my hand enveloped in his as we made our way into his cellar sanctuary. I had about five seconds to catch my breath before he had me pinned to a wall.

Max scraped his scruffy beard over the crook of my neck, his lips exploring my skin as his hand moved down until it squeezed my cock. There was no doubt he was in control here. His grip was firm and certain, like he knew what I needed better than I did.

"This is mine," he said, a hot breath puffing out over my neck as he stroked me.

"Oh my god, yes." It wasn't even a question—and he knew it.

"I want you. I want you more than anything. It hurts, babe. It hurts so bad," he said, his words tumbling out in a gasp.

"Then I'll make it better."

Without further explanation, I backed him across the room until the backs of his legs hit the mattress. I dropped to my knees, edged my fingers under his belt, and pressed my mouth to his fly. I dragged my lips over the denim-covered ridge of him, thick and hard and hot through the fabric. I traced his length down and scraped my teeth over his flared head. His legs shook and he shoved his fingers through my hair as I reversed course and followed him to the root.

"Do that one more time and I'm gonna come in my pants," Max warned. "One more time, Jory. Just you watch."

"Would you like that?" I loosened his belt and unbuttoned his jeans while I asked. I was confident I knew the answer but it wasn't wrong to overcommunicate in these situations. "I want to give you what you want."

Max flailed his arms out. "And I want to give you what *you* want."

"Right. Of course. We're a pair of selfless lovers. That lines up with our track record." I chuckled to myself as I pushed his jeans down. "Let's do it this way. You get this round. I get the next one. Eventually, we'll figure out how to share a round. All good?" I didn't wait for him to agree. "Great. If you had to choose between a dry hump with you coming in your pants or a blow job with you coming in my mouth—"

"That one," he interrupted, slapping an invisible buzzer like he was on a game show. "Second option. Yes, please."

I yanked his boxer briefs down, and his heavy cock swung free. I studied him for a moment, taking in the veins along his shaft, his wide, ruddy head, and his earthy scent. "Good choice."

"If you stare at me like that another minute, I'm gonna come all over your face, babe."

I took pity on his poor, needy cock, curling my fingers

around his shaft and brushing my lips over the crown. "Are you trying to tell me something about your endurance, Coach?"

Max's hands shifted from my head to my shoulders. "More of that," he ordered. "*More.*"

I could've teased him. Could've drawn this out. Could've pushed him to the point of begging. But I didn't want any of that tonight. Begging and teasing had their place but I wanted to *love* him tonight. Even if I wasn't quite ready to say those words, I wanted him to feel it.

"Again, again, again," he chanted. "Please."

"Anything you want, it's yours," I whispered, laving my tongue over him. "Sit down. You're going to enjoy this."

Max's backside hit the mattress with Pavlovian speed. "I'm already enjoying it."

I pushed his clothes all the way down to his ankles and tugged them free. "Come on. Don't set a low bar for me."

"I'm not," he said, his words soft as he watched me settling between his legs, sliding my palms over his bare thighs. "This is perfect, Jory. You're perfect."

I took his cock in hand because I didn't want this to be about the things we said to each other anyway. I wanted him to feel the things I wasn't adept at putting into words and I wanted him to accept them as if I'd said them, shouted them, screamed them into cold, stone-carved truth.

Max's hands moved over my shoulders, up my neck, and into my hair, his body vibrating as I worked him. I swallowed him down and groaned around his girth. The scents of body wash and musk mingled with the rich, salty taste of him on my tongue. I worked him hard and took him deep even as tears filled my eyes and spilled over.

When I slipped a hand between his legs to cup his sac, he tightened his hold on my hair. He shifted a bit, scooting his backside right to the edge. *Ahhhh*. That was where he wanted my attention.

"Jory, Jory, Jory, I'm, oh my god, yes," he stammered, his words running together as I swept a finger over his back channel. His spine arched as he growled low and loud at the ceiling. "I'm—*ohmygod*—yes."

Since I wasn't letting this end after a few brief moments, I bobbed my head in agreement as I shifted from quick, intense strokes to a slower yet equally intense rhythm.

"Ohhh."

I glanced up through the gag-tears and watched Max drop his head back, his face angled toward the ceiling and his chest heaving. Even with lights on, it was shadowy down here, but I couldn't miss the flush coloring his cheeks and neck. He was so damn beautiful. I wanted to tell him that. I wanted him to know he was the best thing I'd ever had at my mercy, the best thing by far, and I'd do this forever if he let me. I'd fall to the ground and let this enormous bear of a man take everything he needed from me, let him use me in any way he wanted so long as it was my name that never left his lips.

I wanted to tell him all of this but I couldn't. Even if

those words glowed in my head like neon signs, I didn't know how to speak them. All I could do was go on teasing, sucking, stroking. Praying these emotions traveled through skin and muscle. Praying he knew.

Though the angle wouldn't allow me to pull off this move for long, I pushed a finger inside him as I swallowed him to the root. A hoarse, wheezing sound rattled out of him and he tightened his grip on my hair like he was in terrible pain but that first, ripe taste of salt promised he wasn't in any form of pain.

"I've heard about this," Max said through clenched teeth.

Since I had a very large dick in my mouth, my response came in the form of raised eyebrows.

"This is the marriage blow job," he continued, one hand on my head and the other braced behind him on the bed as his hips jerked up to fuck my face. "The blow job that's so good it ends in a proposal."

There were gag-tears streaming down my face and I was going to have a cowlick tomorrow from all this hair pulling but I managed to smile as his cock shuttled in and out of my mouth.

"That's okay, Jory. I know you. I know you didn't plan it this way," he drawled. "I'm not even sad you beat me to it."

I managed a jerky nod as he surged forward, locking me in place with his hand on the back of my head. I didn't know what he meant about beating him to something but there wasn't time to examine all these stray comments as he cursed and exploded down my throat.

It was a full minute of him filling my mouth, holding me steady, humming and gasping and vibrating as if unbound electricity was coursing through him. It was *a lot*. I was no blow job master. I knew what I was doing, but I didn't know how to be comfortable with my tear-stained cheeks or my swollen, reddened mouth or the painful erection trapped under cruelly slim trousers that I wouldn't be able to disguise when pushing to my feet.

I didn't know how to embrace the ugly side of sex, the side that wasn't ugly or awkward or shameful at all. If it was anything, it was the human side and that was what I didn't know how to embrace.

Not until Max Murphy cupped my cheeks in his hands, thumbed away my tears, and said, "I love you. No, I don't want you to say anything. I don't want you to say a single word because I know you're not ready for words but I love you. Someday, I'm gonna marry your ass off. You just tell me when you're ready for that."

I bobbed my head. "Okay."

He grinned, big and warm and dazed, and hauled me onto the bed. "Let's get you naked. I'm not finished with you yet."

6

MAX

THE DRIVE from Boston to Sugarloaf, way up in the Carrabassett Valley of Maine, was stupidly long. Really, truly, stupidly long. At several points during those four and a half hours, I suggested we pull off the highway and find somewhere else to hide away for the next seven days, somewhere we could be *now*.

Jory thought I was joking. He laughed and smiled and nuzzled his head against my shoulder while I scowled at the road. He filled the time by thinking aloud about the seventh grade physics unit he planned to launch in January and the new coding initiative he was working on with Juliana. There was also an extensive recap of the holiday spent with his mom and sister, both of whom were epic pains in the ass while he was back home.

"Keaton's biggest problem—well, no, she has a lot of problems. I can't narrow it down to one," he said with a sharp laugh. "Her problem at the moment is wanting to control everyone. Their thoughts and feelings too."

"Good luck with that," I replied, doing my level best at listening and responding while every inch of my body was cranked all the way up.

The only relief was Jory's body on mine, his mouth, his skin, his touch. I wanted everything and I wanted it *now*. It'd been like this since the holiday party. Every minute since, I'd wanted to go crazy on him. The night we'd spent together satisfied about one percent of my needs, leaving me to throb and ache like the thirsty horndog he'd turned me into.

Part of the problem was sleeping with him—actually sleeping—was the best thing in the world. Just the best. And that was a problem because I didn't get to do it nearly enough.

The other part was I *loved* this man and he didn't freak out when I told him. I'd expected some wide-eyed over-whelm and a frantic response (in Jory's careful, controlled way of being frantic) about our relationship moving too quickly, especially after I popped on that part about marrying his ass off. Instead, he'd lit up like the Vegas strip and nodded as if he loved me too. Like he wanted me to marry his ass off.

Being married to him would be real nice. I could already see his crisp button-down shirts lined up in the closet beside my polo shirts. That was the one that always got me. Our shirts in the closet together. I didn't know why it mattered so much but something about sharing a closet and getting dressed together was too right. I could see myself making toast for him in the morning. I'd always make his toast just the way he liked it and I'd smile at the ring on my finger as I slathered that toast in peanut butter.

"I know, right?" He shot me a glance and I nodded because it seemed like the right thing to do even though I wasn't sure where we were in this conversation. "Only Keaton can determine how someone should react to a situation, and god help you if you have an unapproved reaction. I mean, she wants everyone to be happy and joyful because it's Christmas, but she doesn't actually want to do anything to contribute to the happiness or joy. She just wants everyone to be together at the house—and that's it. She doesn't want to do any activities, doesn't want to go anywhere, doesn't want to have people over. And she gets upset when I leave to visit friends, as if that's some kind of knock on her. Basically, she wants everyone to sit around, doing nothing and going nowhere, and brand it a merry Christmas."

"And why do you think that is?" I asked. I'd learned that one from Mal.

"She doesn't know how to experience happiness or joy." He said it slowly, as if he'd realized this right now. "At the same time, she's less of a headache than my mother. Good grief. All she wanted to do was needle me about Bayside."

I glanced over at him. "Why?"

He unscrewed the cap of his glass water bottle and took a sip. "She thinks—and has thought since the start— teaching at Bayside is a huge mistake. She believes in traditional district schools and, in some cases, parochial schools. She doesn't believe in independent schools that aren't tied to a faith and she certainly doesn't believe in charter schools."

Again, I had to ask, "Why?"

Gesturing with his water bottle, he replied, "She's a diehard union gal and she came up in a time when unions made a significant difference in working conditions for teachers. Not that they don't now but it's different." He shrugged, downed another mouthful of water. "Times have changed but her mindset hasn't. She says working at schools like Bayside is asking for trouble." He ran a hand down his thigh, cocked his head to the side. "As if the school will shut down in the middle of the night and we'll come to work in the morning to find the doors barred. Or that we're choosing to get screwed in contract negotiations and pension programs."

"Huh. None of that has ever occurred to me," I said. "Should it?"

"Nah. Not worth stressing over. She's mostly bitter about me choosing something different. Kind of like Keaton, if I don't follow my mother's exact plan of going nowhere and doing nothing, I'm offending her. That's half the reason I wanted to move to Boston in the first place. I had to do something because it was right for me and not because anyone else approved."

I reached over and took Jory's hand. "I'm sorry you had such a rough time at home, babe. I don't want you dealing with that."

"Home is such a complex place for me. I want to go there, I want to visit, I want to spend time with my family. For the most part, those visits are positive. I love my family. My sister tells me horror stories about her clients and my mother fills me in on all the gossip. She's been teaching fourth grade long enough to have the children of her previous students in her classes now, so she knows everyone and everything they're doing. I love all of that. I love making lobster pie with Mom for Christmas Eve and doing Keat's giftwrapping for her because she cannot wrap to save her life. But I hate being made to feel guilty for wanting to spend time with friends or choosing a job that's a good fit for me."

"If it makes you feel any better, holidays at Mallori's house are like being aboard a runaway train. You know it's gonna crash soon enough, but you just don't know when."

Jory shifted in his seat and crossed his arms over his chest as he eyed me. "I need to know more about this. It will make me feel so much better about dropping my family dramas on you."

I blew out a ragged breath and frowned at the road. Why weren't we there yet? Why couldn't we hash out our family dysfunctions later? Right around the time we were too loose and wrung out to do anything but melt into the mattress.

"Mal and her husband do a really good job at making a nice holiday for the kids. They work hard at creating traditions and keeping the magic alive. But Mal needs a phone call from our mother on Christmas. She's not okay if she doesn't get that phone call. She watches the clock all day and if she hasn't heard from Mom by one or two o'clock, she starts coming apart. You can actually see it happening."

"I take it your mom doesn't always call," Jory said.

I shook my head. "Nope. After Mal and I were out of high school, she quit her job and sold her house. She always told us she'd do it, that she'd tear out on her own when we were grown. We never took her seriously. It sounded more like the bullshit you say to keep yourself going than an actual plan, but she did it. She said something about spending twenty years being a mom, eighteen of those years as a single mom, and it being her turn to take care of herself."

"When you zoom all the way out, it makes complete sense. Being a single parent with two kids and working full-time leaves little, if any, room for someone to have a life outside those responsibilities."

"I get that," I said, defensive for no good reason. "It's different when you live it."

"Believe me, I know. The saving grace for my mom was being a teacher. We went to school with her in the morning and we did homework in her classroom in the afternoon. Our schedules were always in sync so Keat and I basically folded into her life rather than her life revolving around us. That setup saved her, but it slapped us on both sides." He drummed his fingertips on his knee. "Where did your mom go? What did she do when she decided she was done?"

"She got rid of everything—Mal will never forgive her for that, by the way—and hit the road." I glanced over at Jory, found him sitting sideways in his seat, his legs folded under him and elbows propped on his knees. "She bounced around for some time but works on a cruise ship now. Dealing blackjack. Yeah, she fuckin' loves it too."

"Though cruise ships don't have the best cell service when they're at sea," he said.

"They don't, and Mom doesn't always remember to check in on birthdays or holidays," I added. "Mal takes it very personally."

"And how do you take it?"

I jerked a shoulder up. "It doesn't bother me, and yeah, I've wondered whether it's strange that it doesn't bother me, but I'm okay. My mom was rock solid when we were kids. She worked her ass off without letting on how tough it was for her. I'm cool with her doing her thing now."

"See? That's the energy my mother needs in her life," Jory said. "Oh—look! That's our turn off."

He pointed at the Sugarloaf sign up ahead and everything inside me grew hot and tight, as if my clothes and skin were about to melt away. I should've admired the scenery since we'd traveled all the way here for it, but this week away was the equivalent of my prom night. There were tons of important things—the location, the outfits, the music—but the only *essential* things were the after-party and the hurried, fumbling sex it promised.

"Thank god," I muttered.

The painful, depressing idea of this vacation resembling a moment of unsupervised teenage freedom wasn't lost on me. I loved my sister for taking me in and helping me get my life sorted out rent-free, but damn, I hated feeling like a kid with helicopter parents circling over-head. I knew Mallori's attentive gaze came from a place of concern—and I knew she simply did not know how to turn it off.

It wasn't like Jory and I *never* had time to be alone together. On certain Saturdays, the kids had back-to-back soccer games which freed up a fine chunk of the day for depravity. Last month, Jory's roommate Claude went out of town for a night, and we had the greatest sleepover of all time because it featured sex, snuggles, and showers.

There were select occasions when Jory spent the night with me too, but he didn't love that setup, which was totally fair. The last thing anyone needed to hear when they were getting dicked down was Mallori yelling for her kids to clean up the Lego disaster they'd left all over the kitchen floor or the resulting complaints from those kids.

No one needed that. No one at all.

The final minutes of our journey stretched on like hours. When we finally arrived, my heart thumped in my chest so hard I was positive he could hear it.

I took Jory's hand and led him into the cabin, barely stopping to abandon our bags, shoes, and winter coats in a heap near the door. We didn't say anything as we headed for the narrow hall I was certain led to a bedroom, though I didn't care whether it was a broom closet or bathroom as I was getting Jory naked either way.

Thank god, it *was* a bedroom.

In the far, far back of my mind, I registered the wide windows facing the ski slopes, a stone fireplace with a plush, fuzzy rug in front of it, and a four-poster bed constructed of thick, knotty pine. All good things and yet none of it was my concern at the moment.

Jory shifted toward the windows, gazing up at the mountain as if he'd never seen anything like it. I stepped up behind him and slipped my arms around his torso. I held him that way for a brief moment because that was all I could bear. I'd waited so long and I didn't think I could wait a minute more.

"It's beautiful here," he said softly.

I reached for his belt. "Mmhmm." When I had it unbuckled and whipped free from its loops, I tossed it to the side. Buttons and zippers followed, then a sweater pulled over his head and denim pushed down to the floor. I pressed my lips to the back of his neck. "You're beautiful here."

He turned his head to the side only enough for me to catch his bashful grin. He watched as I tore off my clothes, his hooded gaze raking over my skin as more of it was revealed. "See something you like?" I asked.

"Like? No." He gave a small shake of his head as he shifted to face me. Then he reached out and tucked his finger under the band of my boxers. He dragged that finger from one hip to the other, a smug smile splitting his face while I groaned in desperate, panting agony. "I see something I love."

A growl rumbled up in my chest as I wrapped my hand around his forearm and yanked him up against me. His breath was coming in quick, rough pants and his skin was so smooth and warm and I was going a little crazy. I couldn't stop hearing "something I love" in my head, couldn't get close enough to him, couldn't give him all the love I wanted to share fast enough.

"Off," I said, pushing at his boxer briefs. "I want these off."

"Then take them off," Jory replied.

If I was a different kind of guy, I'd use this moment to say something meaningful or romantic. I'd promise to love him and protect him always. I'd reiterate my intention to marry his ass off. But I wasn't that kind of guy, the one who put his thoughts into a tidy order and used all the pretty words the right way. I was the guy who stripped off my man's undies like they were on fire and backed him to the bed, then flattened him against the billowy blankets and took his cock in my mouth.

I held nothing back as I sucked him deep and hard. He rolled his hips up, his backside lifting off the bed as he fucked my mouth. He watched me the whole time, his heavy-lidded stare tracking every twist of my fist down his shaft, every wet caress of my tongue over his head, every brush of my fingers along his crease. He watched it all with his lips parted as if he was about to say something, but the only sounds he made were low, breathy sighs and murmurs.

Then—"Ohhh, *fuck*," he groaned. "Fuck, I love you."

The only answer I could offer to that was sliding a finger into his ass and taking him all the way down my throat until my nose brushed his belly.

"Not like this, not like this," he chanted. "Inside me. I want to come with you inside me. Now."

I peered up at him from between his strong, slender legs. "It tastes like you want this."

He draped his forearm over his eyes as he groaned. "Of course, I want this. But I want your cock in my ass even more. I want to say I love you like that, Max."

That did it. That fucking did it. I thought I'd manage, that I'd get through this without tripping over my feelings. But he'd said it two and a half times now—the first one was iffy—and if he said it again, I wouldn't be able to hold myself together.

I hooked my arm under his backside and pillowed my cheek on the heated skin of his inner thighs. He smelled like sex and soap, and I loved him so much. Jory Hayzer was the best. The very best. And the only one I wanted. "I would've waited years. Years. You know that, right?"

Jory pushed up, his brows arched and his shaft bobbing in my face as he shifted. "Waited years for what, babe?" He rubbed his fingers down the back of my neck, my shoulders. "What are we talking about?"

I tipped my head to the side to get a better look at him. "I would've waited as long as you needed because I know you need a little more time. With the love stuff and all. And I thought it would be years. I'd prepared myself for that."

He hummed to himself as he slipped his fingers through my hair. "And I went blurting it out on you."

I dragged my lips over the silky skin between his legs. "You make that sound like an apology. No apologies. I just want to love you now. Want to keep you."

Jory reached for me, urging me up, onto the bed, on

top of him. "I believe I was begging for that just a minute ago."

I pressed a kiss to the corner of his mouth. "You mean it? You really love me? You're ready for the full force of Maximum lovin'?"

"You're so fucking cute when you fish for compliments." He hooked his ankles at the small of my back. "Yes, I really mean it. Have you known me to say things I don't mean?"

I braced myself on my forearms and rocked my shaft over Jory's. At first, he laughed, but then he went cross-eyed and moaned every naughty word he knew. I did it again. "How about the time you hated everything but didn't mention it until we were eating tacos at one in the morning?"

He dug his heels into my ass. "Will I ever live that down?"

"Eventually, yes." I reached between us, took our erections in hand. "Thank you. For loving me."

"Loving you is the easy part," he replied, his lips parted and his eyes still crossed as I stroked us. "Speaking the words is where it gets dicey."

"Are you freaking out?"

He shook his head. "Not about saying it, no. About you edging me for the past ten minutes? Oh, yeah, I'm freaking out over that. I might cry if you keep doing this."

I offered him another rough stroke before saying, "Not until you tell me why now. Why are you able to say the words now? What happened?"

Since I reveled keeping Jory in a bit of agony, I ran my

free hand down his flank and brushed my fingertips over the tender spot behind his knee. A shiver started at his shoulders and snaked down his body.

"I wanted to tell you the night of Tom's holiday party," he started, "but I didn't know how to say it."

With one finger, I traced the seam of his knee again. My touch was light as hell, but Jory went wild for these teases. It turned him on like crazy. "Mmhmm," I murmured against his neck, still dragging my finger over his skin. The rhythm was slow yet deliberate. It promised I'd tease him elsewhere very soon.

His breath was hot on my shoulder when he said, "I realized somewhere in the last month that I craved you in my life. It wasn't even sexual—"

I gave his cock a rude jerk and shifted to stare down at him. "What was that?"

Jory looped his arm around my neck and dragged me down for a kiss. "Believe me, I crave you in very sexual ways. I spent the entire trip bitching about my mother to prevent myself from begging you to stroke me off while you drove."

Dropping my forehead to his sternum as all the blood in my body arrowed down to my crotch, I murmured, "Shouldn't have told me that."

"Oh, stop it. You love it when I'm slutty."

"Like you wouldn't believe," I said.

"What I meant is, I crave your presence in my life," he continued. "Your dick too, don't get me wrong, but it's more than that. I like being with you, and I like who I am when we're together. You never make me feel small or difficult. You work hard at allowing me to experience my emotions, even when they're fucking ridiculous. You make me laugh, and you give me space to be myself. And I love that you've given me all that while also being such an amazing guy on top of it."

I wanted to take all of those words and stow them away for a time when I needed them to fill me, make me whole. I wanted that because I couldn't hear them and keep them right now. Not the way they'd been intended. No, my brain was fixed on sex—nasty, sweaty sex that was over in an eye blink because it was that aggressive—and had no use for those kinds of words. They were too precious for the likes of me, too easy to crush and lose forever.

"To answer your question, I realized this when I was home," he continued. "I wanted you to be there with me more than anything else. I didn't want to be away from you, and I didn't want to be cautious about my feelings anymore."

And since this was so much, *so much*, I shifted away from Jory under the pretense of dragging my lips over his rib cage, licking and kissing as I passed each ridge. "You're so fucking gorgeous," I whispered to his skin.

"And you like that?" he asked. "That I'm gorgeous?"

I nodded, my beard scruff scraping over his flank. Goosebumps rippled over his perfect skin. "Love it," I murmured. "Love you."

For the first time since ducking away, I glanced back at him. His eyes were screwed shut and his mouth open on a silent sigh. His cock was jutting out from his body, thick and throbbing, the head shiny with a drop of arousal. I stroked him once, twice, not nearly as intense as he wanted. Then, I climbed off the bed.

"You *cannot* leave me like this," Jory wailed. "Have you seen what you've done to me?"

"Be good while I'm gone."

I strolled out of the room as if I wasn't a fleshy bag of pulsating need and my cock wasn't thwacking my belly with each step. It looked like I was taking my sweet time, but the truth was, I needed to catch my breath and get a handle on this situation. Had to remember I was the boss. And I had to stop myself from begging Jory to marry me *immediately*.

Once I had the protection, the supplies, and the mindset necessary, I returned to find Jory kneeling on the bed, his cock staring straight at me while he pulled back the blankets and sheets. His face was still twisted in snarling, sexy desire and it damn near dropped me.

I pointed to the bed. "Hands and knees, babe. Show me that gorgeous ass."

"That kind of flattery will get you everywhere," he replied as he settled into position on the center of the bed.

I didn't look up as I rolled the condom over my shaft. "That's good, since I plan on getting you everywhere."

I tossed a brand-new bottle of lube on the bed, climbed up behind Jory, and locked my hands on his hips. I gave him a meaningful squeeze and smoothed my hands down his back and over his ass, my thumbs sliding between his crease with enough pressure to force a shuddering breath from him.

"Doin' all right, baby?" I asked as I grabbed his backside. My fingertips pressed into his soft skin as I gripped and separated him.

"You know how I'm doing," he grumbled.

I tightened my hold on his cheeks, holding him apart. "Mmhmm. I do." Then, I swiped my tongue over his crease.

A deep, guttural groan was his only response. That, and the furious way he balled the sheets in his fists as I teased him with my tongue. I hadn't planned on making him wait, but this was too good. I wanted a bite of that ass and I was going to get it.

Once he was shaking all over and cursing like it was the only language he knew, I reached between his legs, gripped his shaft. "I could spend all day on this ass."

He dropped his head down, between his outstretched arms, saying, "Tell me what I have to do to get your dick."

I pressed a kiss to the base of his spine as I blindly patted the mattress for the lube. Once I found it, I gave him one last torturous lick before drizzling the liquid between his cheeks. It was a fine distraction from the incessant clanging inside my head to claim this man, to make him mine and keep him for always.

"Ready?" I asked, two fingers pushing into his back channel.

"Just fuck me. Please, Max, *please*." He squirmed against my fingers, but quickly found a comfortable rhythm. "I want you like this, Max. I want you a little evil, a little rough, and all the love. I want—"

Jory choked on those words as I pushed into him. A

little evil, a little rough, and all the love. That was what he wanted and that was how I gave it to him. At this point, I couldn't do much else. My cock was as hard as stone and the hot clasp of his body burned straight through the rubber.

And since I was brittle and worn down in certain spots and needed to hear the words he'd promised, I asked, "Is this what you wanted?"

He responded with, "Fuck fuck fuck *fuuuuuuuuck* oh my fuck yes."

I settled both hands on his waist as I rocked into him, my body gaining speed as I bottomed out. "This won't last long, my love."

He reached back, dug his fingers into my thigh. "I love you. I fucking *love* you."

Without thought, my hips snapped forward, fucking him farther up the bed. I shifted my hand to the graceful line of his spine and followed it up to the base of his neck. I pressed his shoulders down to the mattress with the heel of my palm, and held him there as those words sank into my brittle, worn down spots.

"Fuck me like you love me, Max," he said, and that was when everything changed. When everything below my belly button twisted and twisted and twisted. When my skin started conducting electricity. When it seemed like I was hearing from underwater.

Reaching around his flank, I took Jory's erection in hand. "Do it. Show me what you want. Show me how you want me to love you, baby."

And, yeah. My man went wild.

He didn't say anything but he bucked his hips and jackhammered into my fist while I thrust into him. He took everything I gave him and begged for more without saying a word. In fact, I wasn't certain he *could* speak as he was grunting and moaning into the mattress in the most adorably helpless way.

Yet he snaked a hand down and curled his fingers around mine, and something inside me popped open. I didn't know what it was, or whether medical attention would be necessary, but it was open now and I didn't think I wanted it closed.

At once, the pressure of our hands layered together, his tight body, and his freely offered words gathered into a snowball and set off my release. It snapped through me like a whip, eye-wateringly sharp before it smarted and throbbed, everything hot, hot, hot. So hot. So sharp. So much.

I heard him cry out and moan, I heard him scream my name like no man had ever screamed it before, I heard his promise of love, and then I felt his body quake and soften beneath mine. My cock gave another spurt as I ran my hands over him, squeezing and massaging as I gathered him up in my arms. He growled and sighed as I stroked him. There was an occasional giggle when I found an overly sensitive spot.

The condom required tending and Jory needed a warm washcloth for the damp spot on his belly, but I figured that business could wait a minute or two.

"No one's ever said that to me before," I confessed. "No one's ever told me they loved me."

Jory inclined his head to the side, glancing over his shoulder with sleepy, sated eyes. "You mean during sex. No one's ever said it during sex."

I shook my head. "Not during sex. Not…ever."

He blinked. Blinked again. It seemed like he was trying to find something polite to say, the way people did when conversations turned awkward and they didn't know what to do with the discomfort. But then he said, "They missed out on someone special because loving you is the easiest thing I've ever done and all I do is make things more complicated than they need to be."

A laugh from deep in my belly bubbled up and I tightened my hold on him. "No, you don't," I replied. "You make things exactly as hard as they need to be."

He snorted. "I see what you did there."

"Yeah? You caught that one?"

"Couldn't have missed it," he said. "And here I was, thinking your jokes were all about balls."

PART IV

SPRING

"YOU'RE GOING to be fine, babe," Max said. "I swear it."

He'd uttered some variation of that a half dozen times this morning and while I wanted to believe him, I couldn't. We didn't usually meet up before school but the days were brighter and longer now, and at the moment, I was too nervous to sleep, so we'd found ourselves at Max's favorite juice bar every morning this week.

My mother would say this was another one of my anxious quirks, the variety that harkened all the way back to my childhood. Whenever I had an exam or a big event on the horizon, I'd work myself into a frenzy days beforehand, too worried to sleep or eat or pause all that internal chaos to take a proper breath.

I was better about containing it now because my students didn't wait for a slow-moving anxiety attack to pass. Choosing this profession meant learning how to cope in real time as I couldn't walk out on my class to ground myself or breathe through a tough moment. But containment and coping weren't the same as banishment. There were no miracle cures. Anxiety still chewed me up inside like a private tornado, often spinning and churning while I carried on instruction, conducted lab experiments, and talked students through their own crises.

My year-end evaluation with the school principal made for one hell of a tornado.

Seeing as I couldn't hide anything from Max and had long since stopped trying, he knew I was concerned about my eval meeting. He listened to me dissect the lesson I'd taught during my formal observation, when the principal sat in the back of my classroom and took notes on everything I did for fifty minutes. He allowed me to catalog all the ways I could've done better. He nodded along while I hypothesized about the feedback I'd receive in the debrief. But he drew the line when I started wondering out loud about not receiving a teaching contract for next year.

This frenzy wasn't without reason.

In all my years of teaching, this was the point when I'd learn I was being moved to a different grade, a different course, a different classroom, a different school in the district. It didn't matter whether I had a great year because teaching assignments were primarily influenced by teacher seniority, student enrollment, and budgets. Even if I was the greatest middle school science teacher in the entire world, money got the first and last vote in public education.

Things were different here at Bayside, considering this was an independent lab school and we didn't rely on local taxes to determine our annual budget. Some more differences: no seniority, no tenure, no traditional contracts with hard-fought layers of due process against termination on a whim. That—not me moving ninety minutes away—continued to be my mother's biggest hang-up about me teaching at Bayside.

She was an active member in her teacher's education association and had been for decades. She believed in salary scales, pension systems, and collective bargaining. She also believed I was making an enormous mistake by coming here and walking away from all of those employment protections. According to my mother, bopping around grades and courses and buildings was to be expected. I had to wait my turn. Eventually, I'd earn myself a spot that wasn't subject to last-in, first-out rules, and then I'd have everything I wanted. There was no sense wringing hands over it.

As if my hand-wringing ever made sense.

"I don't think there's ever been a teacher who didn't have their contract renewed at the end of their first year. A few decided they didn't want to return and I think Lauren appreciated them coming to that decision on their own but—"

"What if I'm supposed to come to that decision on my own?"

"You're not," he replied with more calm than I'd ever experienced in my life. "You're awesome. Everyone loves you. The kids say you're supportive but strict and they *respect* that. The middle school team would walk out in protest if you weren't renewed, and I bet the elementary teachers would follow too. You're good at this, Hayzer. Damn good. Knock off that defeated attitude because taking the field expecting to lose is the fastest way to make those dreams come true. Get your head in the game and plan to win, you hear me?"

I gave him a watery smile. "Thanks, Coach."

"Don't thank me," he replied, still in locker room pep talk mode. "Kick some ass and then you can thank me."

"I will," I promised.

As quick as a finger snap, he shifted back into my large, lovable bear, saying, "We'll need to celebrate. Maybe we should plan a weekend away before the summer season gets going and everything costs a thousand dollars a night. Maybe Mystic, down in Connecticut. Or somewhere on the coast of Maine. I know a fisherman up there. I bet he'd have some recommendations."

"Yeah," I said, swirling the straw in my green smoothie. Max always made a quip about me going green for science when I ordered this drink. He always had something warm and generous to say, always an inside joke or a funny little thing. "I'd like that."

My mother was wrong. Nothing about this was a mistake.

"SO, JORY," Lauren started as she dropped into the seat across the table from me, "how has this year been for you?"

I laced my fingers together on the table, slowly bobbing my head in acknowledgment as I gathered the right response. Questions like these were akin to conspiracy theories—they made my brain extra twitchy as I tried to figure what they were *really* about and they made it impossible to separate the signal from the noise. It was too easy to answer the wrong way. The trick was replying in some general, factual manner and forcing the person asking to react.

This was one of the reasons why anxiety was so exhausting. Every thought was actually four thoughts. Or more.

After a pause, I said, "I've learned a lot here, and I know my students have learned as well."

Lauren's brows shot up and she studied me for a long, excruciating beat. "I'd say your students have excelled, Jory."

"Oh," I managed. "Thank you. For noticing."

"Couldn't miss it if I tried," she said. "This position is a demanding one. Three content areas to prep, students across three different grade levels, a middle school team loaded with strong personalities. All of that plus serving as the instructional model and resource for campus-wide inquiry-based science? If you've learned a lot this year, then it's fair to say *we've* also learned a lot. You've helped us align and transform science instruction at every grade level."

I blinked as my cheeks and neck heated. "Oh. Thank you."

"Of course," she replied. Then, she patted a folder in

front of her. "Okay, now I'd like to talk about something that might seem overwhelming but—"

The hammer had never come down with such a breathtakingly positive introduction. First time for everything.

"—I know it's more work, more time. There's a stipend, of course, though it isn't enormous. I hope you'll consider it."

I snapped my head up. "Wait, what?"

Lauren waved her hands in front of her, saying, "Sorry, I got ahead of myself. I'd like you to officially take on the role of science chairperson."

"Science...chairperson," I repeated.

"Yes. As I'm sure you know, Audrey chairs English language arts, Juliana is responsible for math, Shay and Clark co-chair social studies, civics, and history, and Linling covers humanities. You'll meet with them once a month as well as working with Tara and Drew to coordinate campus-wide collaborative planning and development. Sound good?"

"Um, yeah," I said, frantically trying to catch up with this conversation. "Sounds great."

"Fantastic. Now, there's one more thing I'd like to discuss with you." She gestured to the open folder in front of her and pushed it between us, angling it for us to read the information. "Backed by a major philanthropic organization, a number of universities, school districts, and education think tanks have developed a collaborative body for innovation in STEAM. They are looking to fill a seat in their upcoming cohort with an elementary science teacher, particularly one experienced with inquiry instruction across multiple grade bands. Naturally, I thought of you."

I shifted the folder to get a better look at the information. A year spent learning about the best—and newest—practices in science, technology, engineering, art, and math? And putting it into practice here at Bayside while I learned? Hell yes. I didn't care if I only slept two hours a night next year, I wanted this. I wanted to be an integral part of this school and I wanted to belong here.

Lauren pointed at a few bullet points. "As you'll see, the work is a blend of online, independent study, and in-person. You'll go to ten day-long weekend seminars in Cambridge over the course of the year plus several school observation visits around the city. We'll take care of getting your classes covered on the days you're off-site. Selfishly, I get the benefit of you coming back from these seminars and visits and training us on everything you learn but I also think this would be super fun for you. I think it's right up your alley."

"I'm honored you thought of me," I replied. "I'd love to go forward."

"Then you'll return? Next year?"

"Was that a question?" I asked on a surprised laugh.

Lauren leaned back, crossed her arms over her torso. "Honestly? Yes. I wasn't sure you would want to stay here or move back to New Hampshire. You wouldn't be the first person to relocate from far less urban areas and immediately want to leave. We've seen a bunch of staff move from western Massachusetts or out in Connecticut and feel like the city was too much, too expensive, too loud, too cramped. I get that, by the way." She motioned to the purple Williams College pennant hanging behind her desk. "It was some epic culture shock coming here after being out in the woods. Aside from the change of scenery, I wasn't sure this setup worked for you. This isn't a traditional district setting like you're used to and it's completely valid to prefer that type of environment."

"I don't want that," I replied, though it wasn't clear what I was rejecting with that statement. This was obvious from my boss's alarmed expression. "Sorry. That came out wrong. Sometimes, I get anxious or over-whelmed, and don't say what I mean."

"I know, Jory. And I know you've modeled real-time coping strategies to our students this year, whether inten-tionally or not. That's important. That's meaningful. Teachers are humans too and their social-emotional expe-riences are as relevant as those of our students. Showing them how to name their feelings and work through them is one of the most lasting lessons you've taught this year. I hope you recognize this as an accomplishment."

I nodded several times because I knew my voice would crack if I spoke right now. I'd always known— even when freaking out over this meeting—that Lauren was fair and deliberate in her leadership, and always concerned with doing right by kids and staff. But now I *knew* it.

"I've never had the same teaching assignment twice," I confessed.

"I know. I hired you, remember? I know where you've

been." She grinned. "I bet it put a tremendous strain on you. I can't imagine bouncing around for years. But all that bouncing turned you into a highly competent teacher. One I'd fight to keep."

"Thank you," I said because nothing else seemed right. "I'd like to stay…and chair the science department. And the STEAM collaborative too. I want to do that."

Lauren closed the folder and pushed it toward me. "That's a relief because I've already submitted your registration forms." She reached for another folder and handed me some stapled papers—a copy of my evaluation. "Now that we have all of that business out of the way, let's talk about the lesson I observed. As you'll see, I found it to be effective and engaging. There's a fabulously long list of things that were very strong, but I bet you're itching to hear everything else. Right?"

I nodded. I wasn't a masochist but my anxious brain struggled to accept positive feedback. Something was always wrong, always in need of improvement. It wasn't that I assumed the worst. No, my brain just believed something bad was always coming my way and I couldn't allow department chair roles and amazing professional learning opportunities to seduce me away from the kind of vigilance required to stay mentally safe.

"That's what I thought," she said. "I have a few questions and some simple spots where you could push students to use more content-specific vocabulary and integrate some of the summarization strategies they've learned in Kerrin's history classes. That strategy translates beautifully between science and history, so you should lean into that wherever possible. Ready to dig in?"

My brain was anxious and I fell into frenzies and there were tornadoes inside me, but more importantly than any of that, I was staying here. That knowledge washed over me like a kettle coming off the heat—it didn't stop whistling right away but the worst of it was over.

Staying meant not packing up my classroom in a few weeks, not driving around with my books and supplies in the trunk of my car all summer because I didn't have space in my apartment. It meant I could find a new apartment, one without a tyrannical roommate, and I could do that without simultaneously looking for a new job. Better yet, I could find a new apartment for me *and Max*. He could finally get out of his sister's basement and we could live together.

What would it be like to fall asleep together *every* night? To share a space all our own? Would we make traditions together, like movie night or meatless Monday? Would we host game nights and dinner parties like his friends and decorate for every little holiday just because we could? Like Pi Day and Star Wars Day and the arrival of the Perseid meteor shower?

Or would we get on each other's nerves? Would our styles and sensibilities clash? Probably not. And if they did, I'd compromise. I'd bend. I didn't care if we decorated our home like a sports bar, I really didn't. My opinions on home furnishings were not nearly as essential to my happiness as Max.

Oh, Max. That man was something special. I'd never

known what it meant to have a partner until he rescued me from that sidewalk last summer. He supported me in the most essential ways, and I wanted to give him as much as he offered me. I needed to do that for him because he did everything for me. Now that I didn't have to pack up and start all over again next year, I could do this. *We* could do this.

"Yeah," I said, nodding. "Let's go."

JORY: It went so well!

Max: I knew it! Great job, babe.

Jory: More good news to share. I'll tell you everything later.

Max: Can't wait. Have an awesome day, babe.

Jory: Love you.

Max: You too.

———

I WAS SUPPOSED to be coaching the track team.

For the most part, I was doing that. "Dale, McKee, Fortunato, Herzgood—this is not a tea party," I shouted while I jogged in place, waiting for the seventh grade stragglers to catch up on our three-mile loop of the streets surrounding the campus. "If you're chatting, you're not running hard enough. Let's go. Pick it up, men!"

But I was also watching the school's side parking lot,

the narrow one reserved for visitors because I caught sight of Jory exiting the building over there. That was weird for a whole bunch of reasons. He was parked in the staff lot—I knew this because I'd followed him here from the juice bar this morning—and he seemed to be waiting for someone. I was far enough away to be wrong about that but there was something about the way he stood, his messenger bag hanging from his shoulder and his gaze tracking each car as it passed.

He didn't mention anything about a meeting after dismissal.

Not that we were planning to hang out this afternoon. I was coaching until five thirty, and Jory liked to maintain a routine of leaving the building no later than five each evening. He went swimming at the YMCA or visited the library to unwind from the day before heading home. His routines were important to him. He would've told me this morning if he was doing something different today.

I continued jogging to keep pace with the team, but I couldn't tear my gaze away from Jory. What was he doing? Why was he waiting there? What—or who—was he waiting for? And why didn't I know about it?

The thing about Jory—and I loved it just as much as I loved the rest of him—was he shared *everything* with me. He hadn't held back since that first night when I dragged him all over town while he grimace-grinned through his misery.

We spoke all the time. Yeah, a good portion of it was phone sex but it was more than that. I knew all the things bubbling up in his head. I knew where he was going and what he was doing because talking it out helped him mentally prepare. We did this almost every night, me in my pull-out bed and him in his apartment. I'd ask, *What do you have going on tomorrow?* and he'd fill me in on all the things cluttering his mind. That way, I could hold his worries and give him a break for the night.

But this was probably nothing. He was waiting for a parent or some other visitor. Maybe a delivery of science-y stuff like beakers and chemicals and creatures for dissection. And though visitors and deliveries always went through the main office without us waiting in the parking lot for them—

"What do we do when we're done, Coach?"

I turned my attention toward the sixth grade speed demon. "Back of the line, Santos. The prize for first place is an extra lap."

As I glanced back to Jory, I nearly stumbled over my own feet when I found him—Jesus Christ—walking into some dude's open arms.

What the literal fuck was that?

I gathered myself, righting my stride and finding my breath in time to watch him cross the parking lot with this guy and—*holy shit*—get inside a high-end electric car.

"What now, Coach?" Santos shouted.

"I don't fuckin' know," I muttered to myself.

"OKAY. LET'S UNPACK THIS," Mallori said as I paced the length of her kitchen. "Maybe he's planning a surprise for you. Yeah! Have you considered that? Maybe he didn't tell you because it's a surprise."

"And he was *hugging* some guy because why? That's not the kind of surprise I want."

Mallori rolled a mug of tea between her palms. "That is...not something I can easily explain." Before I could jump in, she continued, "But it's probably nothing. How do you know it wasn't his brother?"

"Because he doesn't have a brother."

"Uncle, cousin, stepdad, stockbroker, frat brother, minister. Could be anyone he knows in a deep, *friendly* way. It doesn't have to be sinister, Max."

Just this morning he was riding the struggle bus about his eval meeting and now he was secretly running off with strange dudes. Like any of this made sense.

"What am I supposed to do, Mal?"

She frowned down at her tea. "I hate to state the obvious but have you asked him what's going on?"

"And ask what? 'Oh, hey, no big deal but are you cheating on me because it kinda seems like it.'"

"Given everything you've been through, it's a fair assumption to think Jory is cheating."

"Yay for me," I muttered.

"But being fair doesn't make it valid or true," she continued. "The real question is whether you trust Jory. Do you trust him to embrace another man, to get in that man's car with him, to keep a portion of his life private from you? Do you trust him to know beyond a doubt he'd never betray you?"

I didn't know how to answer that. I loved Jory, and I

wanted to believe he'd never, ever hurt me. I wanted to believe I was as precious to him as he was to me. And I wanted to trust him. I really, seriously, wanted to trust him, but everything inside me was frozen solid, braced for impact.

At the same time, I knew this was different. I knew Jory wasn't my ex; he wasn't anything like Teddy. I knew he wanted our relationship to make it—and I knew he didn't have the temperament to go behind my back. The stress of juggling men would eat him alive.

"Since you're struggling with your response to that, here's what I'd recommend," Mallori said. "Communicate. Don't let your mind run away with itself. Call him up and ask—plainly and without hedging—what happened this afternoon."

"Right. Like I can ask him what it was all about without looking like a total creeper for watching it happen from across the street."

"The thing about healthy relationships," Mallori started in that *I know what I'm talking about and you should listen* voice, "is everyone involved has to be willing to make a fool of themselves sometimes. Everyone has to be vulnerable, be comfortable with the discomfort, has to put themselves out there in bare, naked ways."

"Is that so?" I droned. "Why don't you bottle that and sell it on Instagram, then?"

"Such a pain in the ass you are," she muttered. "Go call your boyfriend. I have to get the kids bathed and into bed."

I DIDN'T CALL. I texted.

Nothing big, nothing to show my completely freaked-out hand. Nothing like Mallori recommended.

And an hour later, Jory still hadn't responded.

With most people, this wouldn't have been an issue. With Jory, it was hella strange. Unless he was truly incapable of responding—driving, showering, frying bacon—he always acknowledged messages, even if only to say "I'll get back to you in a bit." He couldn't deal with giving anyone the impression he was ignoring them.

I didn't want to think about why he was truly incapable of responding now. I'd done enough of that with Teddy. I'd let myself imagine what he was doing with those other guys and why he wanted them so much more than he wanted me.

Instead of thinking, I tried to keep myself busy. He'd respond eventually and there was nothing I could do to make time pass more quickly. Watched pots and all. I tidied my room, lifted weights, downed two cups of yogurt while standing in front of the open refrigerator, read a bedtime story to my niece and nephew. I did it all with an eye on my phone, holding my breath for anything.

Not anything, exactly. I'd fully ignored a bunch of school emails, texts from friends, and a wicked good deal on the newest flavors of Built bars.

None of it was what I wanted.

I turned in a helpless circle as I surveyed my basement

confines. This wasn't what I wanted. I didn't want to be here. Not in this basement, not in this holding pattern of in-between life with Teddy and life after Teddy where I was still waiting for those scars to scab over before I could stop gasping and flinching at every unexplained afternoon hug.

I didn't want to be here, not when it meant driving myself up the wall trying to figure out what Jory was hiding from me, why he hadn't told me, and whether I was the kind of man who attracted cheaters. Whether I invited this into my life.

I wanted to finally get on with my life and if Jory wasn't the one because I'd misunderstood everything about him in a major way then I needed to know now. I'd waited too long for—for everything. I couldn't wait any longer.

Without thinking beyond instinct, I dashed up the stairs and out of the house, grabbing my keys along the way and charging toward my car. It didn't occur to me until reaching the sidewalk that I'd forgotten my shoes. That slowed me down but it didn't stop me.

Fuck shoes. Shoes didn't matter. It wasn't like I was walking over hot coals or broken glass. The Quincy neighborhood Jory lived in wasn't that bad.

And—because I wasn't a total beast—I knew my gym bag was in the trunk and I always had an extra set of running shoes in there.

The dashboard clock informed me it was after nine, which was the middle of the night as far as Jory was concerned. On any other day, I'd care about that big time.

I couldn't care about it right now. I couldn't assume responsibility for Jory's needs if it meant displacing mine tonight.

Even if there was a perfectly reasonable explanation for the hug and the car ride and the secrets, this wouldn't work if I allowed myself to sweep away my needs the way I had time after time with Teddy.

Taking care of Jory was one of the most fulfilling parts of my life. It was a purpose and a calling unlike any other I'd experienced. I wanted to be the one to tend to his needs and provide him a quiet place to feel safe and settled because he needed that more than anything else.

I was the one who listened while he unpacked his worries, and I was the one who reminded him to eat, sleep, breathe when the world was too much. I was there when he needed to vent about his mother and sister, politics, and everything else that chafed at him. I did that. I was the one. If he thought someone else could do all that for him, he'd have to tell that to my face.

And my bare feet too.

And he'd do it just as soon as I landed at his front door.

The annoying part of living at Mallori's house west of the city was having to hop on the highway and drive thirty minutes in order to reach Jory's apartment in Quincy. It would've been a million times easier if he lived down the damn street because I was losing my steam with each minute.

Jory lived in a big, fancy house from some historical era, and it had been subdivided (and re-subdivided) into a lot of small apartments over time. It sounded like a nice idea but the whole thing was a pain in the ass. The parking sucked, for one, and the halls were comically narrow and dark. I lived in a basement—if I thought it was dark, it was fuckin' dark. On top of all that, the so-called apartments were a janky mess of chopped-up bedrooms and parlors and shit. The fuses were always blowing and the ventilation was horrible and there was never enough hot water.

Jory should've been living in a decent place with reliable parking and hallways that didn't look like the set of a horror movie. He needed a roommate who wasn't some obnoxious jack-off, someone who didn't make his life ten times more complicated with a load of rules and restrictions.

Now that I thought about it, Jory needed to live with *me*, not in some shoebox with scary halls. If he wasn't cheating on me, I was going to tell him exactly what I thought about this situation and demand some immediate changes.

Yeah. That was a mood. If someone handed me a dish of chocolate ice cream with chocolate jimmies right now, I'd argue about that too.

Because the universe was fucking with me today, I found a parking spot directly outside Jory's building. And since I was dead to rights about this place being totally unacceptable for him, the main door was wedged open with a brick.

It wasn't until I started jogging up the stairs that I realized I'd forgotten my shoes—again.

"Oh, fuck it all," I murmured as I rounded the next landing.

When I reached the third floor, I didn't bother stopping to catch my breath. I banged on the second to last door and rested my hands on my hips.

The door opened, and Claude, Jory's roommate, stood there, glowering at me. "Can I help you?"

"I'm here to see Jory and before you go to the trouble of telling me it's past visiting hours, I'll remind you he pays his rent on time, every time, and does more than his share of the communal chores. One late visitor isn't going to kill you and you know it."

Claude blinked rapidly as his lips parted. "Pardon me but—"

I stepped around him and headed toward Jory's room. I could hear him speaking as I approached but I was running on too much adrenaline to make sense of his words. I knocked once and reached for the doorknob. "Jory. It's me." I hesitated. Then, "I'm coming in."

From the other side of the door, I heard him saying, "Can you hold on a minute?"

I pushed the door open and found him holding a sheaf of papers, his phone pressed to his ear.

"Max, what—where are your shoes?"

"Fuck the shoes," I said, waving off that issue. "You—" For all my fuming on the ride over here, I couldn't remember what I'd meant to say. "You didn't text me back."

He held up a finger, saying into the phone, "I'll call you back. Okay? Yeah. Tonight. I will. Thanks so much."

With that, he turned, set the phone and papers on a small desk tucked into the corner. "I was going to text you back, right after I wrapped up a few things. I was working on something." He pivoted, his hands loose at his sides as he considered me. "I promise, Max. It's not like I can forget about you."

I held out my hands and reached for him but couldn't leave the threshold. "What were you working on?"

Jory dipped his hands into his pockets. He was still dressed in the steel gray khakis and white button-down with tiny blue diamonds from school today. He'd abandoned his tie at some point and the buttons were open at his collar.

I wanted to lean in and lick my way up his throat to his sweet lips. Even when I didn't know what to believe, I still wanted him—and maybe that was what was wrong with me. Maybe I didn't know how to turn off my desire to love someone who I believed to be mine and listen to common sense.

"If I told you," Jory started, "it wouldn't be a surprise."

"Babe, I can't stand any more surprises." I pressed my palms to my eyes then blew out a huge breath as I raked my fingers through my hair. It was standing in a hundred different directions but that didn't matter. "I saw you. This afternoon."

He pushed his glasses up his nose, crinkled his forehead. "Where, exactly?"

I fisted my hands in my hair. "Oh, babe. No. You can't do that to me. Don't make me think about you in multiple situations where I can only assume the worst."

Jory's lips pulled down into a sharp frown. "What do you mean? What are you assuming?"

Sensing Claude was lurking over my shoulder, I stepped inside Jory's room and shut the door behind me. Since there were only a few steps separating us, I leaned back against the door. I required that small bit of distance.

"I saw you hugging someone and then driving off with him." I crossed my arms over my chest. "What am I supposed to assume?"

Jory clapped a hand over his mouth. "Oh my god," he said through his fingers.

"That reaction doesn't help. Babe, I'm not strong when it comes to this. If you want out or—or whatever—I need you to say so. I can't watch you slip away from me, and I can't pretend I don't see it."

He squeezed his eyes shut for a moment before whirling around and snatching some papers off the desk. He crossed the short span between us to stand in front of me. "I wanted this to be a surprise," he said, his gaze not meeting mine. "I wanted to be the one to do something grand and wonderful. I wanted it to be me this time. I wanted to be the hero instead of the one in need of rescue. The one who figured everything out and came up with the big new plan for us. Instead, I've turned it into an actual disaster."

I studied the frames of his tortoiseshell glasses, his thick, dark brows, the slight pink of his cheeks. And I wondered what the hell he was talking about. "Jory, babe, I don't know what you're trying to say."

He pressed his hand to my forearm and held up the

papers. "I'm trying to tell you I found an apartment. For us to live in. Together."

I blinked. That wasn't what I was expecting at all. "You're not banging the guy with the Tesla?"

He reared back, his eyes wide. "Tom? No! Not only would I not do that but his fiancé would literally and truly dismember me."

I snapped my head up as his words struck me—and knocked my noggin against the door. "Fuck, that hurt," I muttered. "Wait a second. That was Tom? When did he get a Tesla?"

"That is not the point," Jory cried. "The point is, you thought I was cheating on you! You should know I'd never do that to you."

"But even when I *know*, and I *should* know, I don't really know," I replied. "It doesn't make sense but it's the only truth I know. I'm learning my way out of this hole but I'm still in it, babe. I'm still scared as hell that I'm not enough to keep someone happy, that there's something wrong with me."

"There's not a single thing wrong with you." Jory pried my arms open and pressed himself against me, tucking his head under my chin the way I liked and gliding his hands over my back in light circles. "You are working through heavy shit, and I'm so proud of you for coming here and asking the hard questions. I know it must've been excruciating to do that and I'm sorry you felt like you had no other option. And I realize it has nothing to do with me, just like my anxiety has nothing to do with you. It's who we are and how we are, and there's nothing wrong with us."

I let him hold me as those words gradually seeped in, as I became aware of the tension between my shoulder blades and up my neck, as I recognized the cool hardwood beneath my feet. My mouth was dry and there was an unavoidable hint of artificial blueberry flavoring on my tongue. Occasional creaks and rustles from the other side of the door told me Claude was still listening in but that didn't matter. I folded my arms around Jory's body and held him close.

"You want us to live together?" I asked.

"Yeah, I do," he replied. "I thought we could get a little place and make it our own. I wanted to get everything set and then surprise you with all my good news but I bungled it instead."

"And Tom? He helped you find an apartment?"

"I texted him this morning, right after my meeting with Lauren." Jory glanced up at me, a slight smirk on his face. "You were right, by the way. Everything went well, and she offered me a contract for next year *and* the position of science chair. Plus, there's a—"

"Science chair? That is amazing, babe," I said, cupping his cheeks in my hands. "I love that for you."

"It's gracious of you to refrain from saying I told you so." He glanced at my mouth, and I leaned in because I couldn't ignore a request like that. But I stopped before our lips met. "It would be good if you kissed me now," he whispered.

"Would it?" I replied. "Do you deserve a kiss because

you had a good day? Or because you want to feel better about the misery I experienced at watching you hug some dude today?"

"He's hardly *some dude*," Jory said under his breath.

"I've spent the past few hours thinking that. It's going to take more than a couple of minutes to unwind it all." I traced the line of his upper lip with my thumb. "I'm starting to think I should make you suffer a bit."

"Promise?" he replied.

I closed the distance between us and captured his mouth with everything I had, all the fear and the love and the old hurts. I tasted him—and that horrible fake blueberry from the yogurt I'd binged—and those hurts didn't ache so much anymore.

Love didn't heal wounds or erase histories. It didn't make any of the bad shit go away or prevent it from coming around again. But love made it easier to stand up to those things. Love was there to lean on when times were tough and it was a soft place to land when the world was overwhelming. Love opened its arms to anxiety and fear and all the other broken bits we carried with us and said, "You can put that down now."

"I'm so sorry you went through these things this afternoon," Jory said between kisses. "I'm sorry I did that to you."

Since I intended to make good on that punishment, the one that wasn't a punishment at all but rather me working out some possessive energy on Jory and him reaping the benefits, I bit his bottom lip and shoved my fingers through his hair. "I'm sorry I reacted this way and busted your surprise. Someday, I won't even blink when I see you hugging a strange guy and getting in a strange car because every single ounce of me will know better than to doubt you're cooking up something good."

"Speaking of which." He tipped his head toward the desk. "The reason I was with Tom and ignoring your texts is he knew of an apartment coming on the market that would be perfect for us. He wanted me to see it today before it was opened up to brokers. And it is, it's perfect for us. Top floor in a triple-decker. The *entire* top floor! Max, seriously, you'd go crazy for this place. It's two bedrooms which is great so we have can have some extra space for an office-slash-exercise-room or something. It has an updated kitchen and new bathrooms *and* in-unit laundry. Off-street parking is included in the rent and there's even a little shared backyard."

"Anywhere is an improvement over Mallori's basement but where is this?"

"It's in Jamaica Plain, right between the Southwest Corridor Park and the Harvard Arboretum. Think about all the walks we could take! You might even convince me to jog one of these days."

I smiled at his sparkling eyes. "There's a library in that neighborhood."

"Oh, I know," he replied. "I could walk to the library, Max. Isn't that incredible?"

"You liked it?"

"So much," he answered, almost breathless. "You would too. I'm sure of it. But Tom needs to know tonight if we want it. He said he can pull some strings and waive some broker magic to get our application in first."

"I love you," I said, punctuating those words with a kiss. "And I want to work at being in love with you for a long time. I want to cheer you on at work, and I want to smack your ass at home every night. I need to get better at trust and be better at boundaries." I gestured to my bare feet and the room around us. "As you can see, I have a lot of work to do there."

Jory laughed as he dropped his forehead to my chest. "I want all of that too."

"Then let's call your secret boyfriend up and get us an apartment," I said.

Despite the fact he was laughing, he said, "That is not funny."

"Maybe not to anyone else but we're allowed a second of dark humor, babe." I surveyed the room as he grabbed his phone. "After you're finished with Tom, you're packing a bag and coming back to Mal's with me. I know it's not awesome in the basement but I want to be with you tonight." I cut a glance toward the door. "And I don't want Claude listening."

Jory made a sour face at the door. "Don't mind him. He's just salty because I told him I'd be moving out this summer."

"You already gave notice? Even before telling me about this apartment? Even before getting the apartment?"

He gave a sweet, boyish shrug that cracked my chest wide open and dug my heart out in one scoop. It was

Jory's now and that was it. "I knew I'd find a way to make this work, and for once, I didn't stop to bleed over every last detail of it."

"What was that like?"

He tipped his chin up, considering this. "Exhilarating. I'm sure the reason I didn't notice you this afternoon was the blind, terrifying exhilaration of it all. Deciding I wanted to find a place for us and then Tom coming back with an availability before lunch—but I had to act today —was wild. All day long, I just kept saying yes. Yes, science chair. Yes, a yearlong STEAM cohort thing. Yes, an apartment in JP. Yes—"

"What STEAM thing is this? You didn't mention that," I interrupted.

He shook his head. "I'll tell you about it later. It's all good news, I promise, but I have to call Tom tonight. I'll cry ugly, snotty tears if we don't get this place. I've already planned an Earth Day party there next spring."

"Take care of business, babe," I said. "Then I'm taking you home with me. It doesn't matter who hears the pull-out bed squeaking tonight."

Jory snorted as he tapped his phone. "I'll remind you it's a school night and I'm going to crash real soon."

"Then I'll give you the little spoon treatment instead. Either way, I'm winning."

PART V

SUMMER

9

JORY

"I CAN'T BELIEVE this is it," Mallori said. She grabbed a fleece blanket from one of Max's laundry baskets and folded it in half, and then folded it again and again until it formed a small rectangle. "I'm going to miss you guys so much."

Moving day was finally here. School was out, I had a couple of weeks before the STEAM collaborative kicked into gear, and we had a bunch of friends coming to help us cart our things to our shiny new Jamaica Plain apartment. The one that was not subterranean, not shared with an anal-retentive demon, and not filled with small children.

"I wouldn't spend too much time with that blanket," Max said as he piled a rainbow of running shoes into another laundry basket. It seemed boxes were not his preference. "I can't tell you the last time it was washed and it's seen a thing or two." He watched as she ran her hands over the nubby fabric. "By a thing or two, I mean penises."

I snorted out a laugh as Mallori dropped the blanket to Max's pull-out bed. We liked to snuggle under that blanket while we watched television. It came in handy when the kids came bounding down the basement stairs without warning.

"Oh my," she grumbled.

"Don't worry," I said to her. "I washed it last week."

Max glanced up from his shoes to shoot a wink in my direction. "Last week was a good time."

"I might not miss this part," Mallori said under her breath. "Will you guys come visit? Promise me you'll visit."

"Of course," I replied as I rolled my ties into neat coils.

"Yeah," Max agreed. "Why wouldn't we leave our sunny new apartment with non-dungeon-y bathrooms and all that unnecessary privacy to come here and get psychoanalyzed for an hour? Don't know about you, Jory, but I can't think of a single reason."

Mallori shook her head but Max didn't notice. He'd moved on to packing the shirts hanging in his closet.

"I know, I know," she said. "You want your space. You deserve that. I get it."

"We will miss you too." I caught her eye from the opposite side of the room and nodded as reassuringly as I could manage. "I mean it, Mal."

No exaggeration there. I'd lived much of the past two months in the garden apartment—as I preferred to call it —and with that came more time with Mallori. I still wasn't comfortable in anyone's home but my own, though this place had come to feel like a place where I belonged. It was also a serious upgrade from my apartment with Claude. I hated paying for something I didn't use, but life was less stressful when I woke up beside Max.

Even if I woke up to the sounds of children screeching at each other over control of the television remote at six o'clock on a Saturday morning.

Even with my things scattered across two apartments, two cars, and my classroom.

Even when all of this upheaval and transition was hell on my anxiety.

"The kids are going to miss you too," she continued.

"The kids are going to miss cockblocking me," Max muttered from the closet.

Mallori rolled her eyes at that and crossed the room, an empty box in hand. "Jory, what am I going to do without you?"

"You're probably going to have to talk to your husband again," Max said. "You remember him, right?"

"When did you get so mouthy?"

He pointed at me. "It's all his fault."

True facts. No sense disputing this.

Mallori circled the room and surveyed our work, her arms folded over her torso as she nodded at each stack of books and boxes. After a considerable pause, she asked, "What am I going to do with this space now?"

Max looked up from his work of folding shirts. "What do you mean?"

She waved her hands between us like that explained everything. "You're not moving back. That's obvious. You're always welcome here, don't get me wrong, but you're with Jory now. You have your first place together, and eventually you'll find another place, and someday, you might decide to get married and—and you're leaving, Max. I'm feeling a whole lot of things about that, but most of all, I'm proud of you." She snatched a pillowcase from one of the laundry baskets and used it to mop the tears from her cheeks. "And you too," she said to me. "I'm so happy it's you. I'm happy you found each other."

I watched Max as a rush of emotions played out on his face. "I guess you're right. This...this is it, huh?" He glanced toward me, a wide, cheeky grin lighting up his face. "You're stuck with me, babe."

Mallori blotted a fresh round of tears, saying, "I'm just going to head upstairs and pack some food for you to take. I don't want you to worry about finding a local grocery store or figuring out which restaurants deliver tonight. You have enough happening. I can take care of this for you."

She continued rattling off a list of reasons she needed to ply us with food, but neither Max nor I were listening.

"Is it real now?" I asked.

He rubbed a hand over the nape of his neck. "Yeah."

"Good-real?" I asked as I approached him. "Or scary-real?"

He leveled me with an impatient glare that said I wasn't to doubt him. "Amazing-real. Totally fucking amazing. I get to start the rest of my life with you. This is it. This is the next adventure, babe. When we look back, we'll talk about the year we dated. *Before* we moved in together. And just like Mal said, we'll have this first place, and then a second place, and as many others as there are after that."

"And then we'll differentiate between *before* you married my ass off and *after*."

He reached for me, locked his arms around my waist, and shoved his hand under my shirt. Just because he could. "That's right."

"What do you think about two summers from now? Not next year, but the year after? That will give me plenty of time to get my ass in shape to be married off."

He shifted his hand down, cupped my backside with a harsh, possessive squeeze. "Are you proposing to me, Hayzer?"

"Only if you're saying yes." Since I couldn't keep anything from this perfect man, I continued, "I thought about it, and the next year will be too busy. I'll be doing the STEAM collaborative, and we'll be figuring out how to live together, and we won't have time to plan a quality party."

"Which is essential," he mused, still grabbing my ass.

"Very. And we need to save money for this party. Plus, our friends and families need plenty of notice. I don't intend to compete with anyone for the ideal wedding date." I pressed my lips together to conceal a wicked grin. "And I like the idea of a long engagement."

"Why is that?"

"Because I want to enjoy this time, this slice of after

dating and before marriage time. I want to have so much fun choosing our venue and sampling cakes and letting everyone gush over us. I want to love every minute of planning the party that will lead to the next part of our life together. And I want everyone to toast us with champagne for months and months."

Max leaned down and pressed his lips to mine. It was a gentle, patient kiss that warmed me all over. "Yes," he whispered. He kissed me again, both hands on my ass now and his shaft rubbing against mine. "I'll marry your ass off, and I'll wait two years to do it because that will make you happy."

"I love you."

"Love you too," he replied. "I have since that very first day. Decided I wanted to keep you close and keep you mine the minute I saw you on that sidewalk."

"And look what you did," I said, waving a hand at the boxes around us. "You made it happen."

He nodded, his nose skimming over mine. "I know."

"Should we tell Mallori? The part about us getting engaged, not that you had some big, confident feelings last summer."

"Let's keep that to ourselves for a few days," he said. "We can't have her crying into all of our pillowcases."

I nodded. "I can agree to that."

Max blinked away, humming to himself. "I guess it's a good thing I saved that lady's card."

"Which lady's card?"

"The one from the pumpkin patch," he said, as if that

made total sense. "The one who wanted to shoot our engagement photos."

There it was. The teeny, tiny reasons that added up to the enormous mountain of reasons why I loved this man. "Yeah, Max," I said as my eyes filled, "it's a good thing."

AN EXCERPT FROM PROFESSIONAL
DEVELOPMENT

They *really* hate each other.
This would be fine except for the issue of them sharing a job title
…and an office
…and now a five-hour-long drive to a conference their boss has made mandatory to resolve their issues.

I couldn't remember whether there was a coffee shop in the hotel lobby. I hadn't paid much attention when we'd arrived last night.

After hours in a confined space with Drew, the only thing I'd cared about was getting away from him. The entire situation was bad enough but after we'd stopped at a sandwich shop for a quick meal, he'd rolled his shirt-sleeves up to his elbows and drove the remainder of the distance with bare forearms.

The audacity of that fucker. Really.

But, with respect to coffee, I knew hiking around

downtown Albany was a possibility. I shrugged on my coat, hoisted my bag to my shoulder, and headed toward the door. I didn't mind leaving the hotel this morning, considering I'd be closed up in a windowless ballroom for the next eight hours and—

—and I walked straight into Drew freakin' Larsen.

"Oh my god, what are you doing here?" I cried, stumbling back against the door and slapping a hand to my galloping heart.

He responded with a slow blink and a scowl that told me he wasn't concerned with the fact he'd scared ten years off my life by lurking outside my room.

He extended his arm toward me and it was then I realized he was holding two cups of coffee. "Here."

I took the cup and examined the order label on the side. Large almond milk latte with extra cinnamon sprinkle. My exact wintertime order. "What—how—I mean—thank you?"

He shook his head as if my gratitude was annoying. Typical. Leave it to Drew, with his impeccably pressed trousers and dress shirt that fit like skin, to blow off the one pleasant word I said to him. If there was justice in the universe, Drew Larsen wouldn't have made clothes look this good.

"Everything about that order sounds terrible," he said, taking off in the direction of the lobby.

I followed but refused to match his near-sprinting strides. We had plenty of time and I required all of it to figure out how he knew how I took my coffee. "And yet you still ordered it."

"Only because I wasn't going to risk arriving late because you require specialty coffee." Drew glanced over his shoulder and realized I was several paces behind him. He stopped, waited for me to reach him. He raised his paper cup before continuing down the hall. "Black."

"Congratulations," I replied. "Unfortunately, the only prize for drinking bitter, boring coffee is the hollow sense of self-importance. I hope you enjoy it."

"You could've just said thank you," he grumbled.

"I did. It was the first thing I said."

"No, you screamed like I was holding a decapitated head rather than a cup of nausea-inspiring coffee," he replied.

"Perhaps I screamed because you were lurking outside my door and that shit is creepy. You could've knocked or even texted me."

"I was *waiting* for you," he snapped. "I didn't want to bother you."

"Oh, so you'd prefer to give me a heart attack first thing in the morning? How kind of you."

"There is no winning with you," he murmured.

"With *me?* You're out of your damn mind if you think *I'm*—"

Drew edged into my space, his hand hovering over the small of my back but never actually touching me as he shuffled me around a corner.

Completely unamused by this morning's antics, I leaned back against the wall and took a sip of my coffee. Cinnamony perfection. He watched me for a second, so damn perturbed by my refusal to take his bullshit seriously.

With his hand flattened on the wall over my shoulder, he leaned down to meet my gaze, his chest nearly brushing mine. "Say thank you."

I arched a brow. "I already did."

"Say it and mean it."

We stared at each other for a moment, the scents of coffee and cinnamon swirling around us.

We hated each other, that was fact. But there were instances like these where I wondered if I understood the full spectrum of hate.

Maybe there were corners of hate that were more than wanting someone to burst into flames or, less fatally, never be able to find a phone charger when they needed it. More than wanting to beat them at every game.

More than any of that, maybe hate wasn't hate at all.

"Tara," he whispered, edging even closer. At this range, I could see the flecks of gold and amber in his eyes and imagine the texture of his dark, close-cut beard. "Say it."

"Thank you for the coffee." There were ten sarcastic, cutting jabs waiting on my tongue but I held them all back as he watched the words moving over my lips like they had shapes and forms he could distinguish from thin air. "Thank you for remembering what I like."

"You're welcome." He stared at me with those dark eyes of his, as if he could see inside me and page through my thoughts. Except he didn't, he couldn't. I didn't allow it. He saw only what he chose and only the worst of me. "We should go. I don't want to be late."

Professional Development is now available.

Tara Treloff and Drew Larsen hate each other.

They ***really*** hate each other.

This would be fine except for the issue of them sharing a job title
…and an office
…and now a five-hour-long drive to a conference their boss has made mandatory to resolve their issues.

And they would've been able to muddle through all of those matters but a major snowstorm is heading their way
…and there's only one bed.

AN EXCERPT FROM FRESH CATCH

If you enjoyed Max and Jory, you'll love Cole and Owen
in *Fresh Catch.*

"May I join you?" I asked, leaning through the doorway to the porch.

Owen was kicked back in his chair, a book in his lap and a tumbler of whiskey by his side. If there wasn't an interesting ball game to watch after dinner, Owen often settled on the porch and I holed up in my room. I'd made good progress with a handful of new ideas I was testing out, but I was climbing the walls tonight.

I didn't mind the routine we had going here-awake before dawn, on the water all day, fish market followed by work fixing up my boat in the afternoon, dinner around sunset, bed shortly after-but I needed something more tonight. Back in California, most of my days were spent talking. Taking calls, sitting in meetings, hearing from my coders, arguing with my board. There was always someone or something that required my attention, and being here with Owen was still strangely quiet for my tastes.

Gesturing to the open seat beside him, Owen said, "Yes, but I have some conditions."

"Anything," I said, dropping into the open rocking chair. Before coming to Talbott's Harbor, I would've ascribed rocking chairs to grandmothers and nurseries, and nothing much else. But these were just right.

"No questions," Owen said. I bit back a groan at that. "You've asked all the questions necessary, and I need a break." I opened my mouth to reply, but he held up his hand. "No. No, this isn't an opportunity to ask why. Just live with it."

"I'll try," I said, rocking back in the chair. I could see why Owen enjoyed this. It was just like being on the water. "It would be really terrible if I died of curiosity, though."

Owen snarled and slammed his book on the table beside him. "How would that even happen, McClish?"

I held out my hands, shrugging. "I can think of a number of ways," I started, "but I'll keep them to myself. I don't want to bother you."

He hissed out a breath and I was convinced he grumbled, "Oh, for fuck's sake."

I had to suck my lips between my teeth and bite down to keep from laughing. "We don't need to talk," I said. "We've got the ocean and the stars, and there's no need to talk. This is great. You do you, Bartlett."

I glanced over at him. He was actively growling, and

that was probably fine for him because he couldn't turn himself on with that sound. I did not possess the same immunity. With my hands folded over my crotch as casually as I could manage, I gazed out over the water and focused on identifying all the constellations I could find. It was good, distracting work, and it would've kept me distracted if not for Cole's huffing and sighing and snarling.

Such a moody one, this Owen Bartlett.

"All right," he said, finally breaking free of his growlfest. "How would one die of curiosity?"

"Marie Curie comes to mind," I mused.

"How do you figure?" Owen snapped. "She discovered radium."

"Oh, yes, and polonium," I agreed. "It killed her."

He reached for his whiskey and took a hearty gulp. "Right. You're not discovering new elements tonight."

I nodded toward him. "And the cat."

Owen waved his glass in front of him. "What cat?"

He was getting riled up, and I loved that shit. A few days ago, I pretended I didn't know the difference between flat head and Phillips head screwdrivers for the simple pleasure of his exaggerated reaction.

"The one killed by curiosity," I replied. "That cat. Poor bastard."

Owen sighed as he shook his head, but it morphed into a chuckle. Soon, his shoulders were shaking as he laughed. I laughed too. I couldn't help it. The deep, fullbodied sound was contagious.

"I don't know about you, McClish," he said as he patted his belly. "I just don't know."

"What do you want to know?" I asked.

He considered his whiskey for a moment before saying, "You're from California? That's where you grew up?" He sipped, and then shot me sharp glance. "It would explain a lot."

"I am," I said carefully. I longed for a drink to occupy my mouth and hands. I hadn't thought that far ahead before venturing out here. "But-I mean-not the California most people associate with California."

Owen regarded me over his glass, an eyebrow bent. "There are multiple Californias?"

I murmured in agreement. "Northern and Southern," I said. "But there's more to it than that. It's a collection of ecosystems more complex than anything contained within conventional notions of statehood." Both of Owen's eyebrows were arching up into his hairline now. "When people think of California, they think of Los Angeles and San Diego. Surfing, beaches, girls rollerskating in bikinis. But that's not the whole story. You have the South Coast but also the North and Central Coasts. There's the Sacramento Valley, the San Joaquin Valley, and The Valley. There's the Cascades, the Sierras, and the Inland Empire. And then there are the big cities. Bay Area, Los Angeles, and San Diego."

"That was an extremely long way of telling me that California is a big place," he said. "This is why you're not allowed to talk."

I leaned toward him and rapped my knuckles on the

arm of his chair. "I forgot about Orange County. Add that to the list."

"Is that where you live?" Owen asked. "Or where you're from?"

I shook my head, laughing. "No and no," I said. "Like I said, people associate California with beaches and bikinis, but that's not how it is for everyone. I grew up about three hours east of San Diego, right along the Colorado River and the Arizona border. It's hot and dry and mostly flat, and the only kind of trouble you can get into out there is stupid trouble."

"You speak from experience," Owen said. "Nearly running your boat aground isn't your first brush with being a damn fool, I take it."

Why did I enjoy this man's insults so much? I couldn't explain it, but I wanted him to keep going. Pick apart my privilege-soaked preferences and deride my expensive polo shirts. Tear down my quirky for the sake of wonky mannerisms. Strip it all away.

"If you're asking whether I hacked into Palo Verde High's student information system and deleted all of my unexcused absences from skipping ninety percent of my calculus classes-" I held up my hands and then let them fall. "Then, yes, I might've found myself in a bit of trouble."

"Of course," Owen muttered.

"But I'll have you know," I added. "I only got caught because I took the final exam. The teacher didn't recognize me. I should've skipped that too, and then hacked back into the SIS to give myself a grade. Should've. Didn't. Me and my goddamn morals."

Owen stared at me for a long moment, his eyes narrowed and his brow crinkled. "Are there any conse- quences in your world, McClish?"

"There are," I said, breaking away from his gaze. "There are definitely consequences." I cleared my throat as I sneaked a glance at him. His attention was on the stars now. "Anyway, I live in Palo Alto."

"Which is in the Bay Area," Owen supplied. "Near San Francisco."

"Right," I said. "My sisters are all over the place. One in Denver, the other outside of Baltimore. My mom lives in Palm Springs now. I tried convincing her to check out Balboa Island or Marina del Rey, but she prefers the inescapable heat. I only visit her in the winter. I can't deal with summer in the desert. I feel like I'm trapped in a dehydrator and turning into beef jerky."

"You'd make for some fine jerky," Owen said, laughing.

"As would you, Bartlett," I replied. There was no humor in my tone, but I couldn't hold back the smile.

"I'd gnaw on you," he continued, eyeing my torso.

My heart was in my throat, thumping fast as I tried to breathe, swallow, think.

What the actual fuck was happening here? Was he...hitting on me?

No. Of course not. This was an awkward bit of humor gone astray, not a revelatory moment where we simulta- neously flashed our queer cards.

Or maybe it was exactly that moment.

"I'm not a piece of jagged, dried out meat," I said indignantly. "I'm tender, juicy meat."

Nothing ventured, nothing gained.

"Yeah, you are." Owen barked out a startled laugh and pushed to his feet. "Whoa. Okay. Now I know I'm drunk," he said. "Get some sleep, McClish. Another early day is coming our way."

I nodded and babbled something in response, but I couldn't stop hearing his words in my head. I'd gnaw on you. It wasn't clear what I'd gained there, but I was satisfied with the venture.

Fresh Catch **is available now!**

Take a vacation, they said. *Get away from Silicon Valley's back-stabbing and power-grabbing. Recharge the innovative batteries. Unwind, then come back stronger than ever.*
Instead, I got lost at sea and fell in love with an anti-social lobsterman.
There's one small issue: Owen Bartlett doesn't know who I am. Who I really am.

*

I don't like people.
I avoid small talk and socializing, and I kick my companions out of bed before the sun rises.
No strings, no promises, no problems.

Until Cole McClish's boat drifts into Talbott's Cove, and I bend all my rules for the sexy sailor.

I don't know Cole's story or what he's running from, but one thing is certain: I'm not letting him run away from me.

ALSO BY KATE CANTERBARY

Benchmarks (Bayside School) Series

Professional Development — Drew and Tara

Orientation — Jory and Max

The Santillians

The Magnolia Chronicles

Boss in the Bedsheets — Ash and Zelda

Walsh Series Spinoff Standalone Novels

Coastal Elite — Jordan and April

Before Girl — Cal and Stella

Missing In Action — Wes and Tom

The Walsh Series

Underneath It All – Matt and Lauren

The Space Between – Patrick and Andy

Necessary Restorations – Sam and Tiel

The Cornerstone – Shannon and Will

Restored — Sam and Tiel

The Spire — Erin and Nick

Preservation — Riley and Alexandra

Thresholds — The Walsh Family

Talbott's Cove

Fresh Catch — Owen and Cole

Hard Pressed — Jackson and Annette

Far Cry — Brooke and JJ

Rough Sketch — Gus and Neera

Get exclusive sneak previews of upcoming releases through Kate's newsletter and private reader group, The Canterbary Tales, on Facebook.

ABOUT KATE

USA Today Bestseller Kate Canterbary writes smart, steamy contemporary romances loaded with heat, heart, and happy ever afters. Kate lives on the New England coast with her husband and daughter.

You can find Kate at www.katecanterbary.com

CPSIA information can be obtained
at www.ICGtesting.com
Printed in the USA
BVHW071226081220
595179BV00001B/130